Mel Bay's

Celtic Encyclopedia
mandolin edition

BY ROBERT BANCALARI

Contents

Irish Music

Airs

Fare Ye Well, Ballinderry

Irish Air

Gallager's Lament

Irish Air

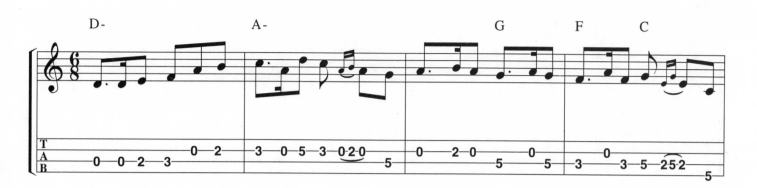

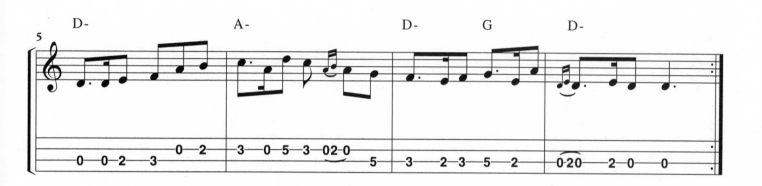

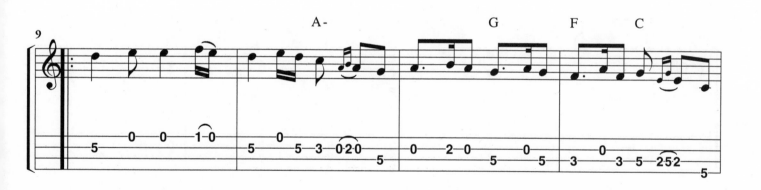

Lament On Con O'Leary's Wife's Death

Irish Air

Milking Song

Irish Air

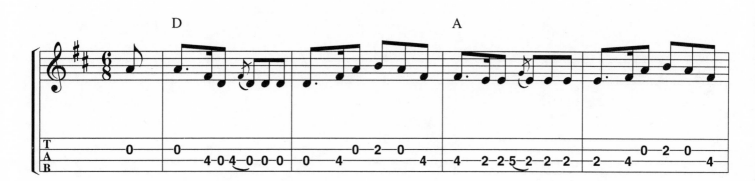

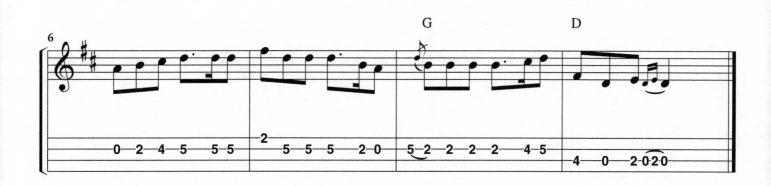

Black-Eyed Susan

Irish Air

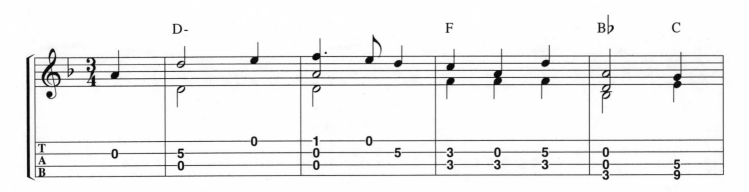

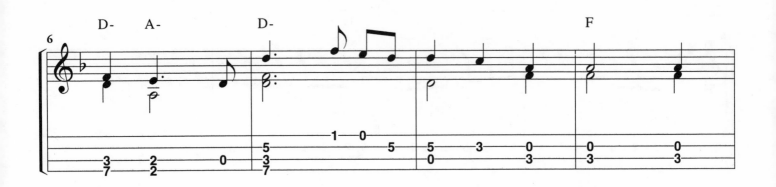

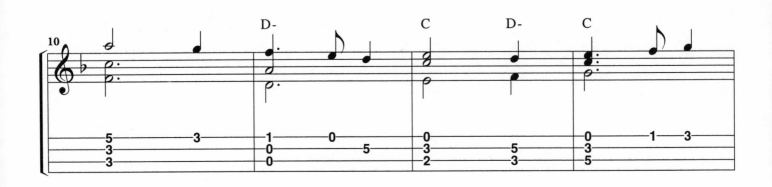

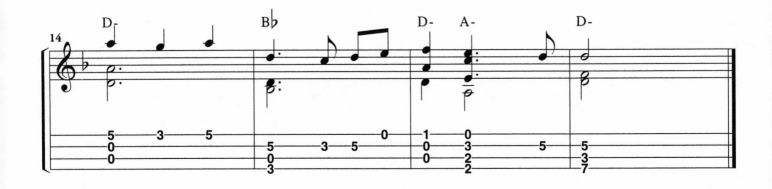

The Handsome Cabin Boy

Irish Air

The Lady and the Farmer

Irish Air

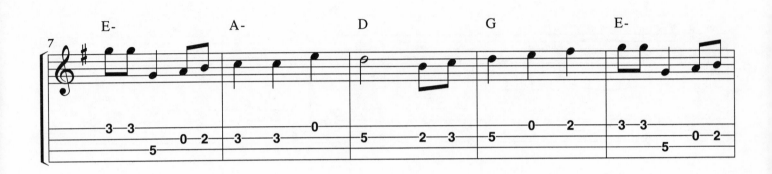

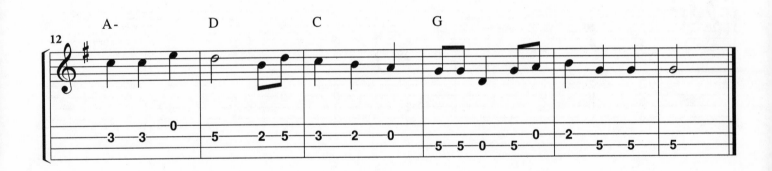

The Fun at Donny Brook

Irish Air

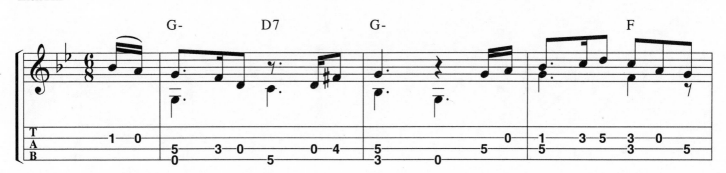

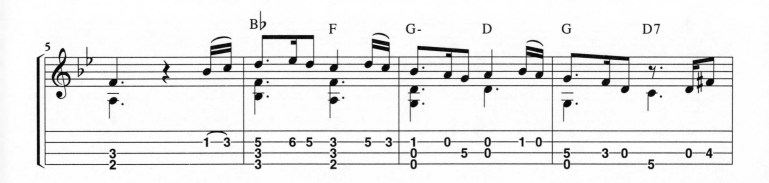

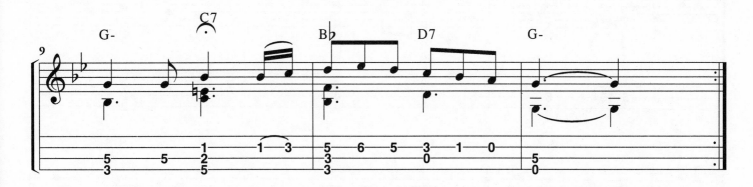

The Friar's Hill

Irish Air

Mary's Return

Irish Air

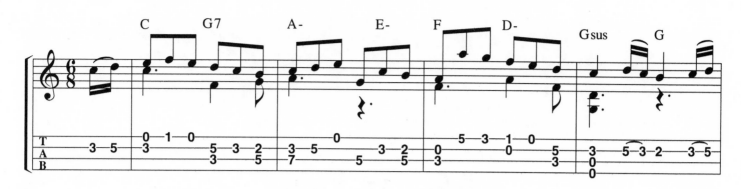

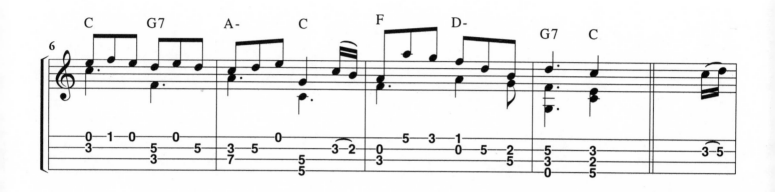

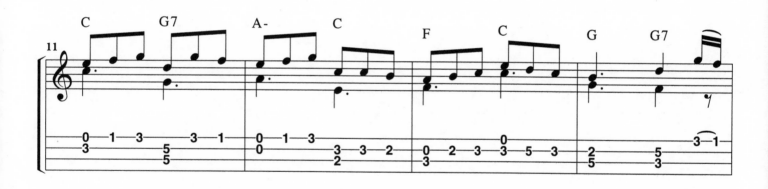

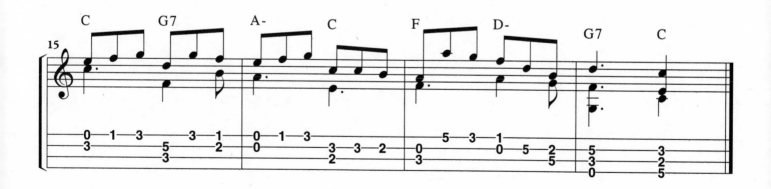

Marches

The Hurler's March

Irish March

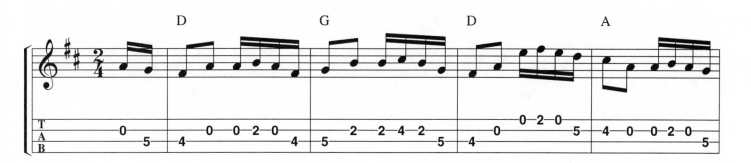

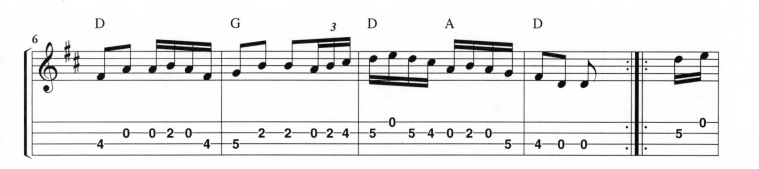

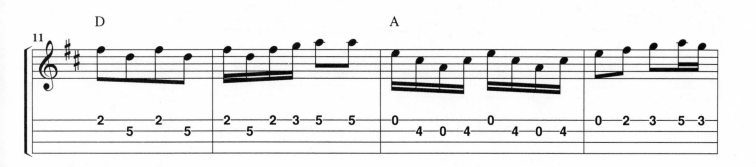

Brian Boru's March

Irish March

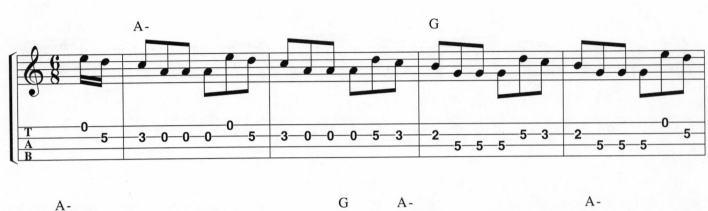

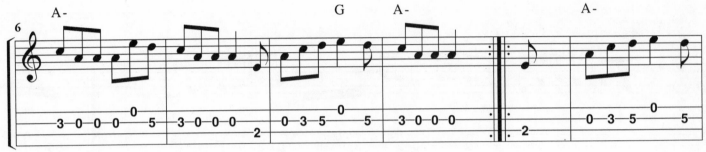

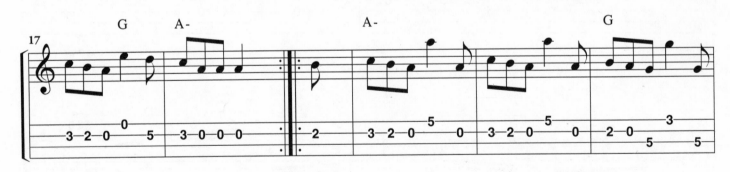

Drocketty's March

Irish March

March

Irish March

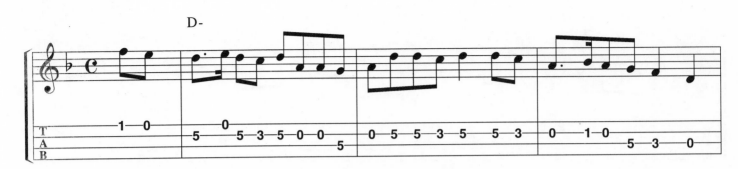

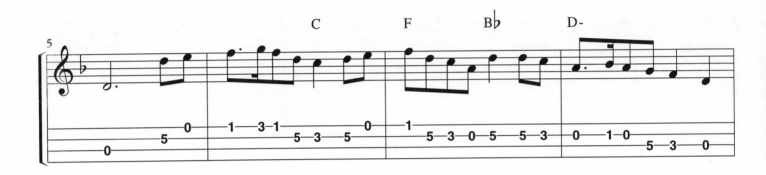

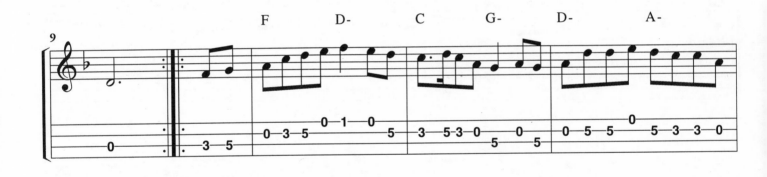

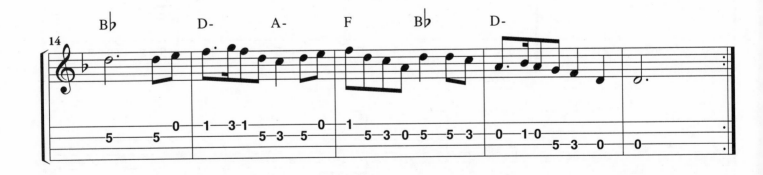

O'Donnell's March

Irish March

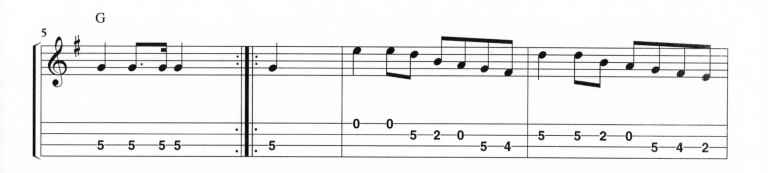

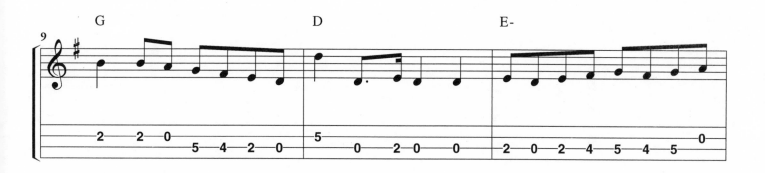

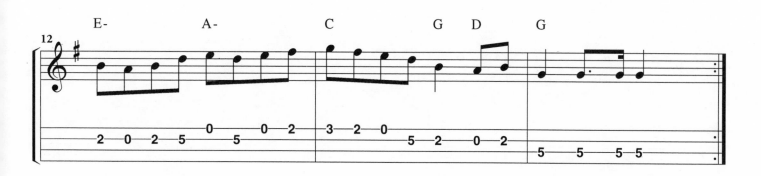

Turlough O'Carolan
(1670-1738)

Planxty Edmond Dodwell

18th Century Irish

Turlough O'Carolan
(1670 - 1738)

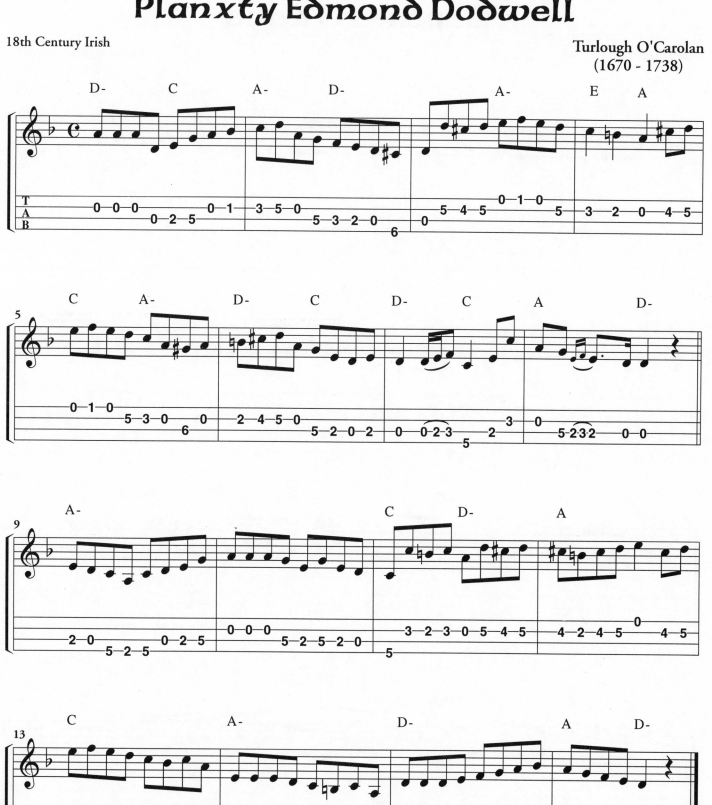

Captain O'Kane

18th Century Irish

Turlough O'Carolan
(1670 - 1738)

Princess Royal

18th Century Irish

Turlough O'Carolan
(1670 - 1738)

Planxty Browne

18th Century Irish

Turlough O'Carolan
(1670 - 1738)

26

Planxty Charles Coote

18th Century Irish

Turlough O'Carolan
(1670 - 1738)

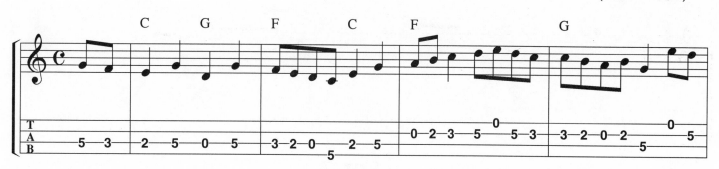

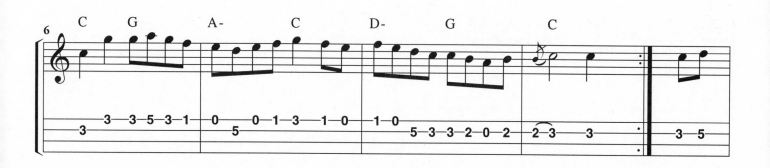

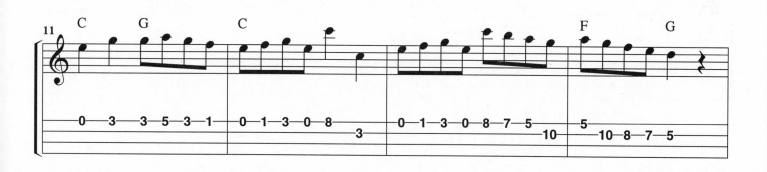

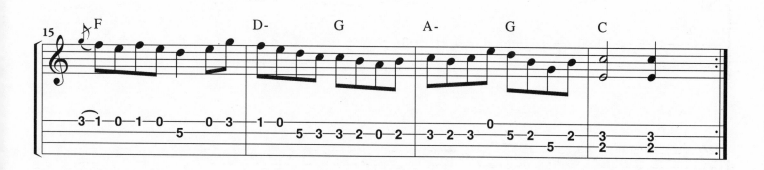

Jigs

The Pipe on the Hob

Irish Jig

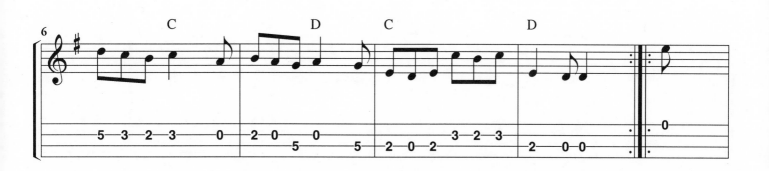

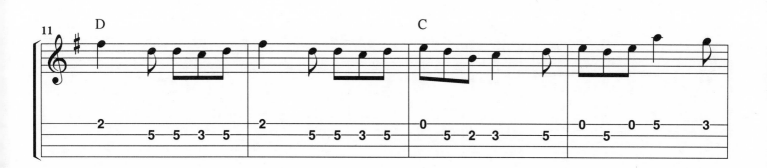

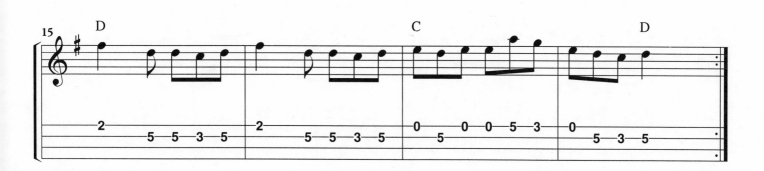

Do You Want Anymore?

Irish Jig

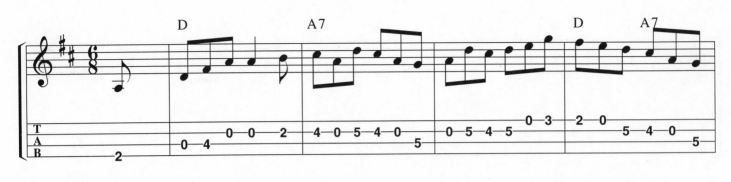

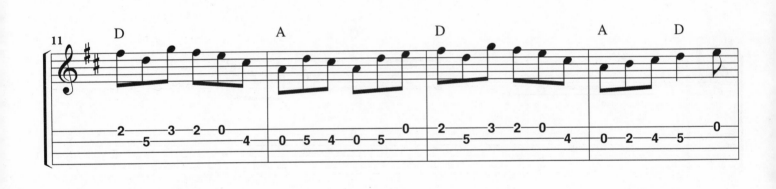

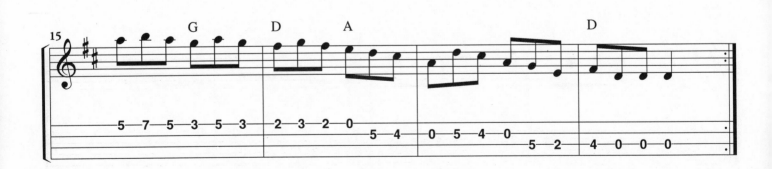

The Mummer's Jig

Irish Jig

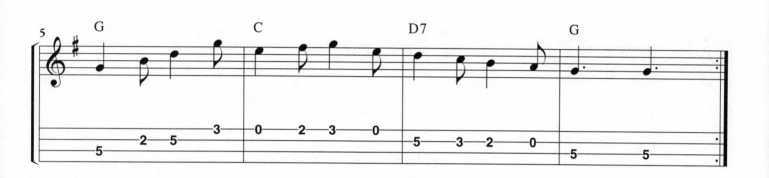

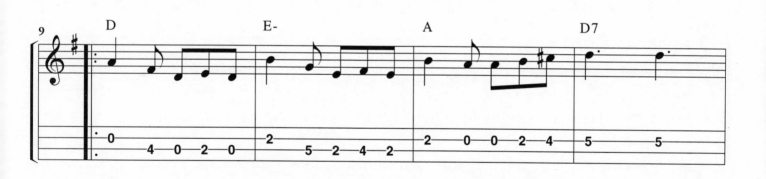

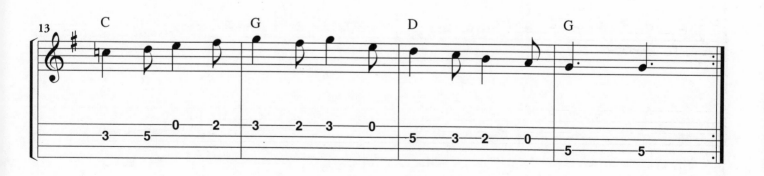

The Redmoor Jig

Irish Jig

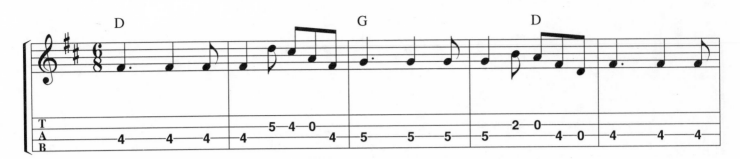

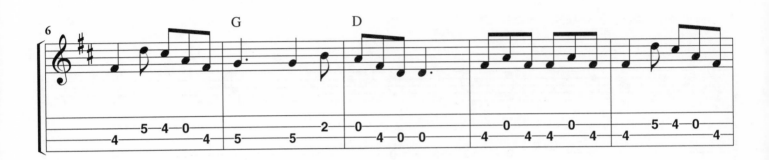

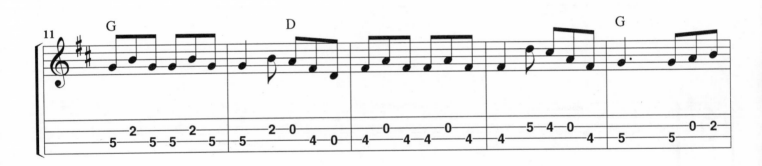

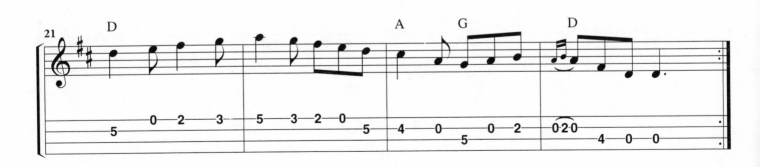

32

The Price of My Pig

Irish Jig

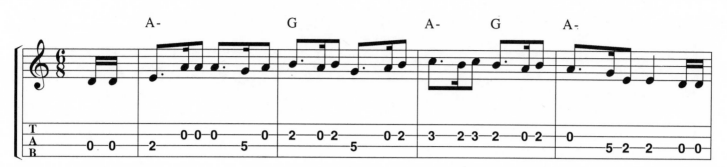

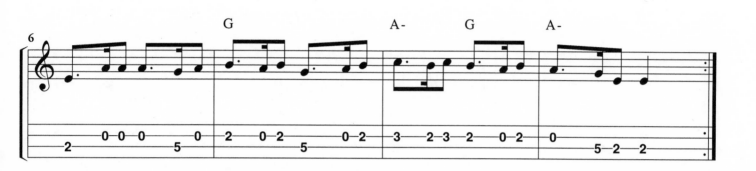

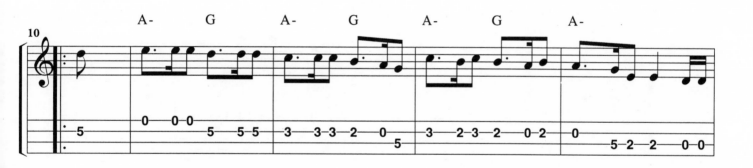

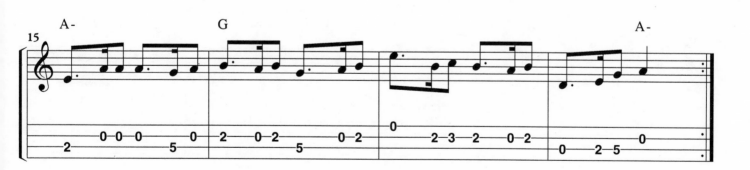

Carman's Jig

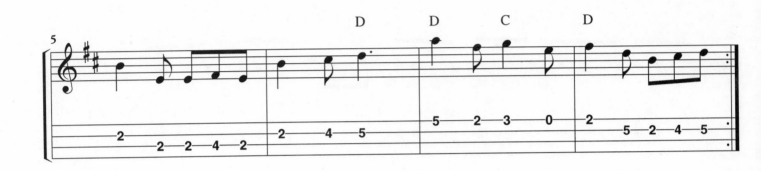

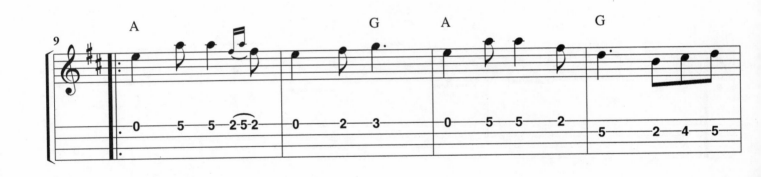

Tom Billy's Jig

Irish Jig

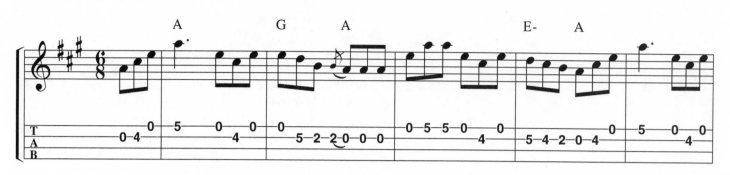

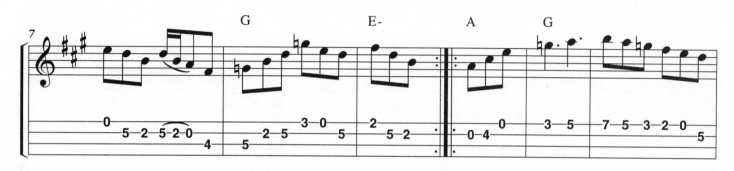

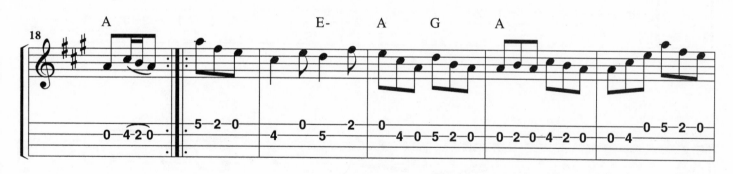

The Boy's of Tralee

Irish Jig

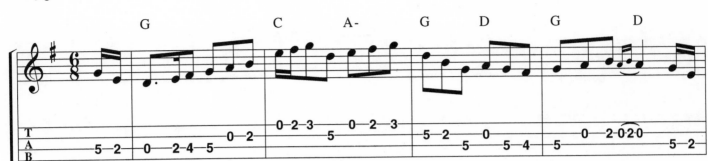

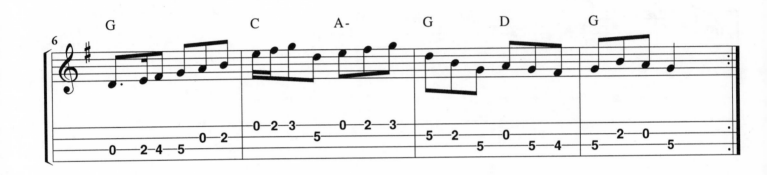

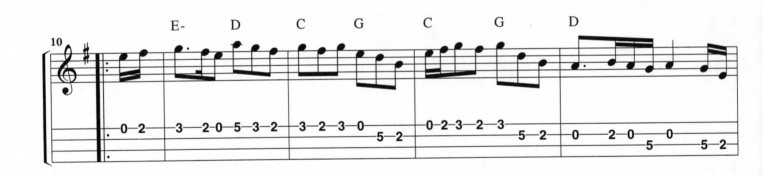

The Madcap

Irish Jig

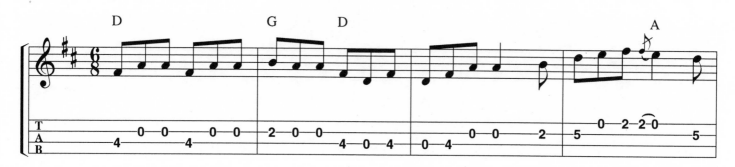

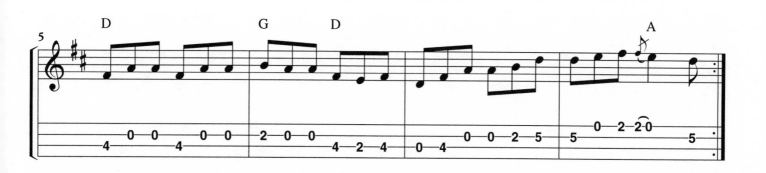

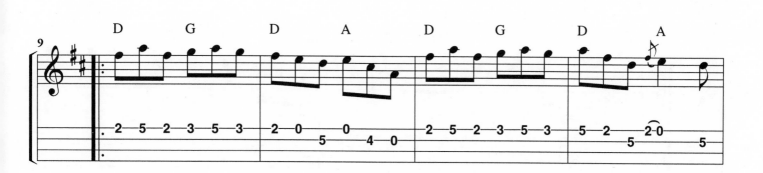

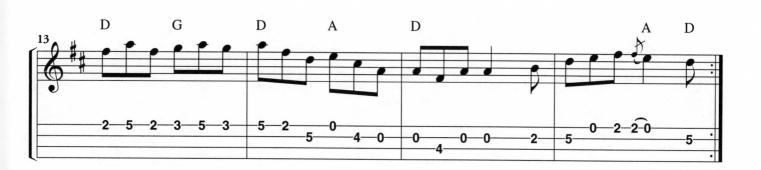

Have a Drink on Me

Irish Jig

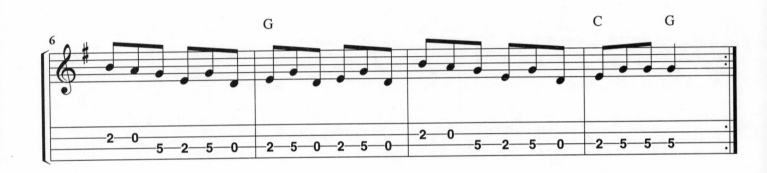

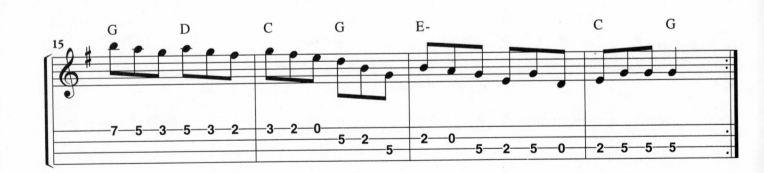

Slip Jigs

Hardiman the Fiddler

Irish Slip Jig

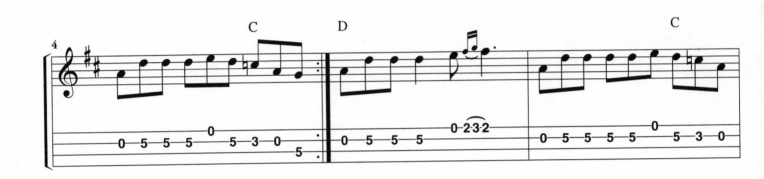

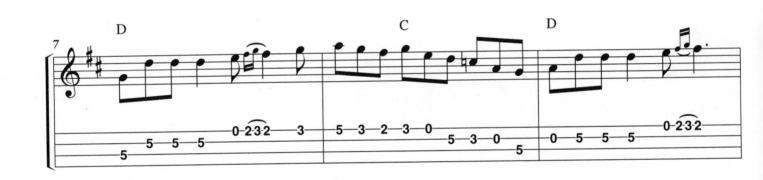

Ellen O'Grady

Irish Slip Jig

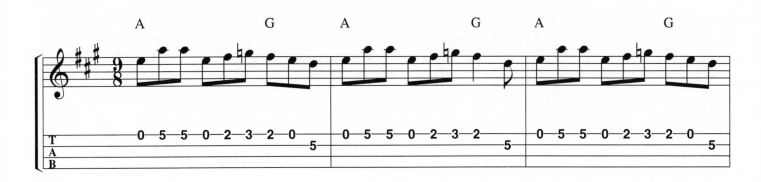

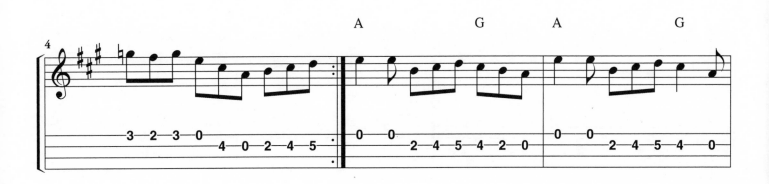

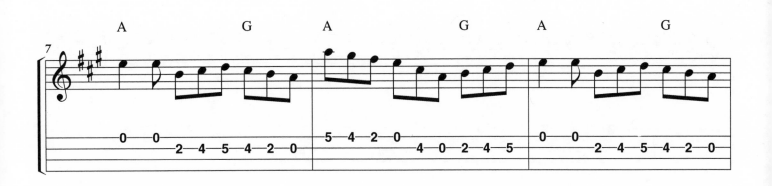

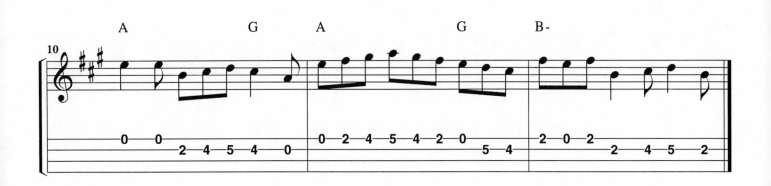

A Blast of Wind

Irish Slip Jig

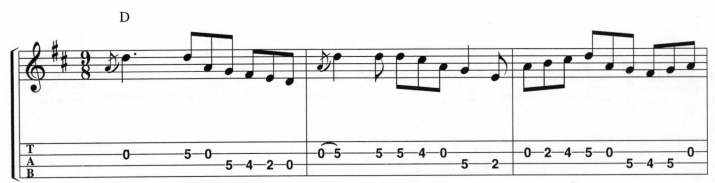

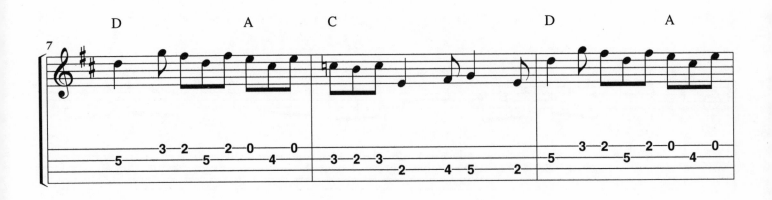

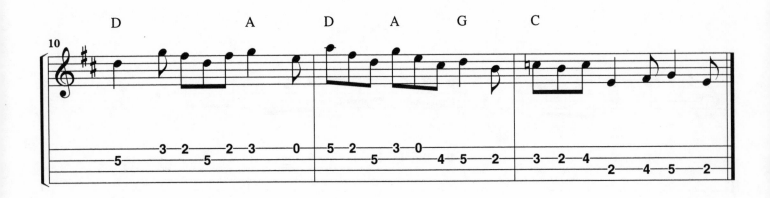

The Sail 'Round the Rocks

Irish Slip Jig

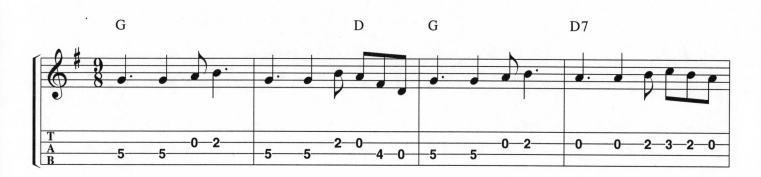

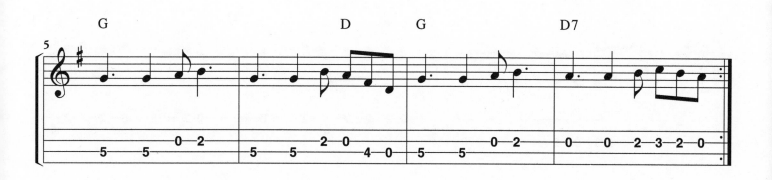

Fox Hunters Jig

Irish Slip Jig

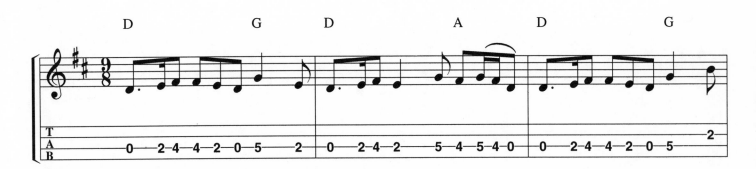

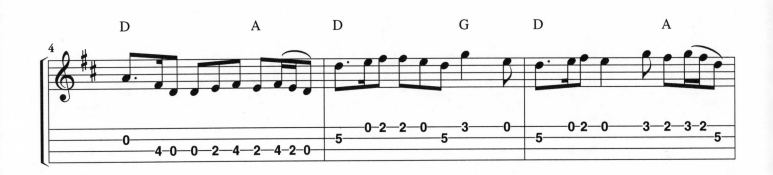

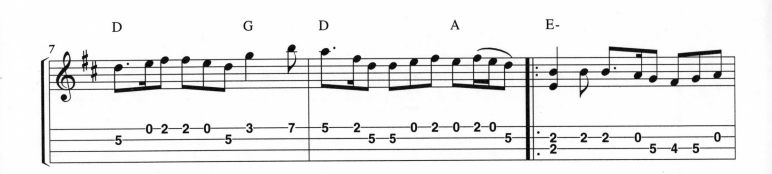

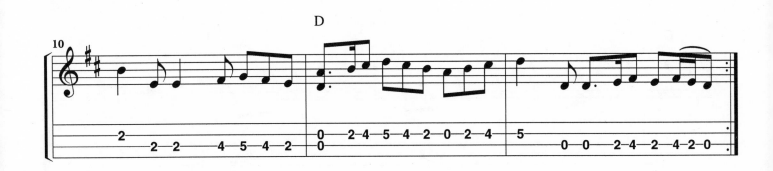

Hornpipes

The Last of the Twins

Irish Hornpipe

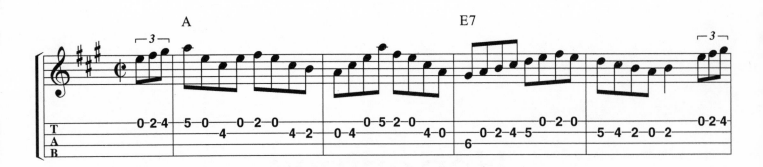

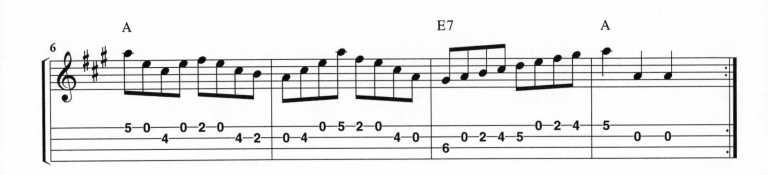

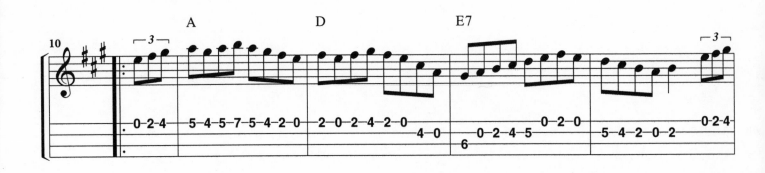

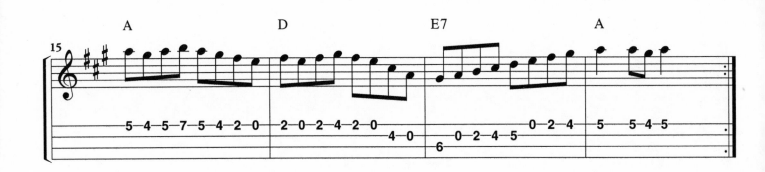

The Maid of Listowell

Irish Hornpipe

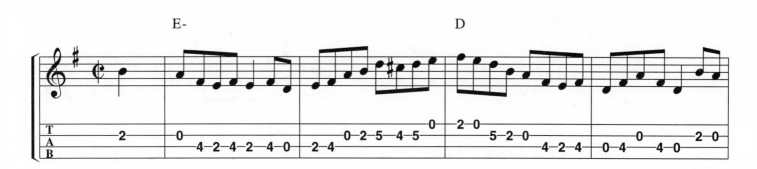

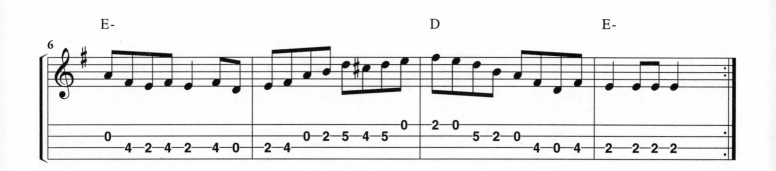

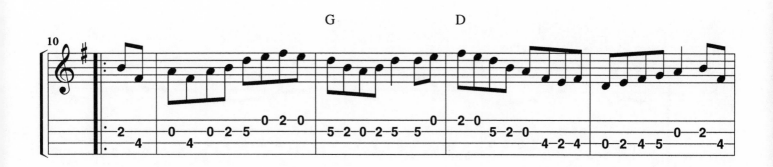

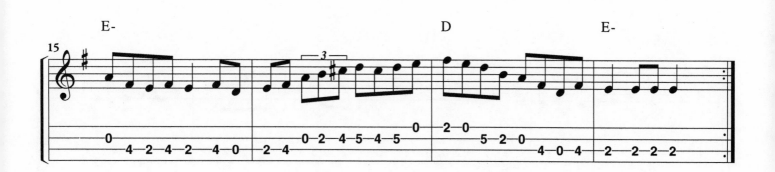

From Galway to Dublin

Irish Hornpipe

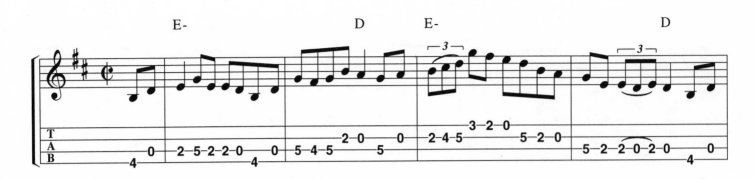

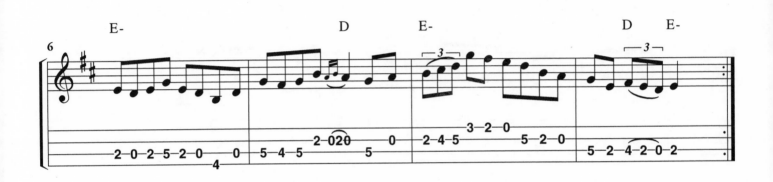

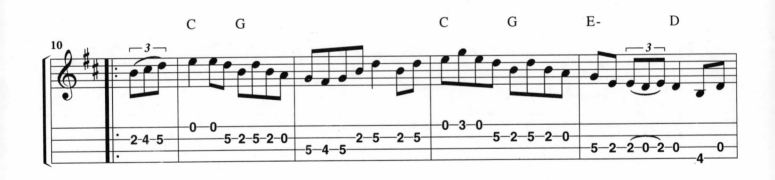

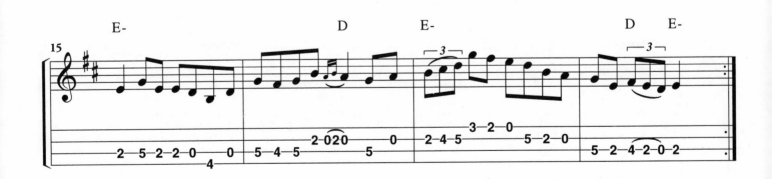

Nelson's Victory

Irish Hornpipe

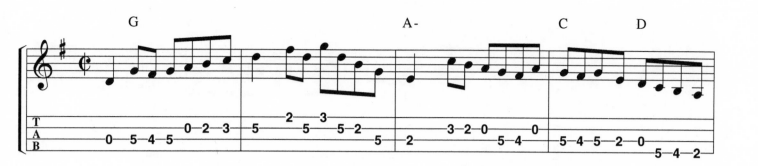

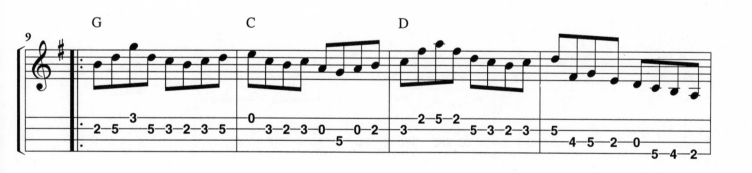

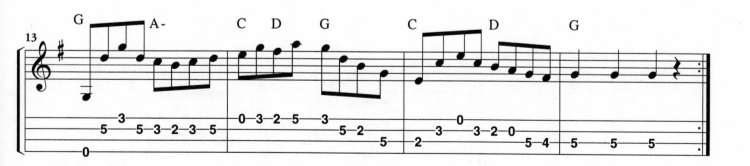

The Harvest Home

Irish Hornpipe

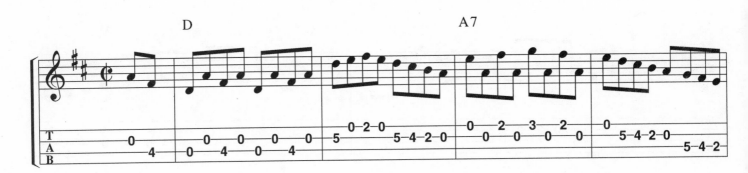

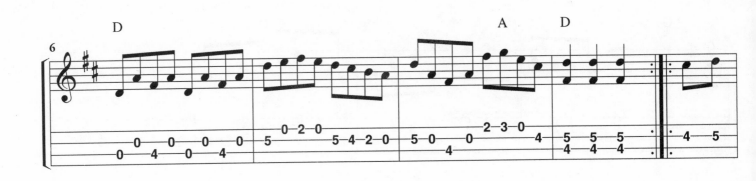

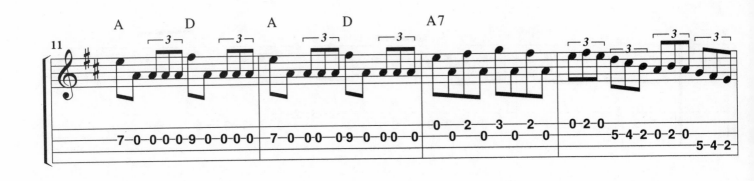

The Mountain Top

Irish Hornpipe

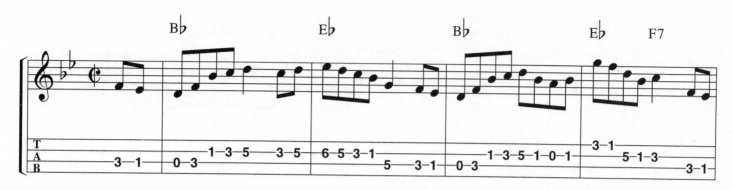

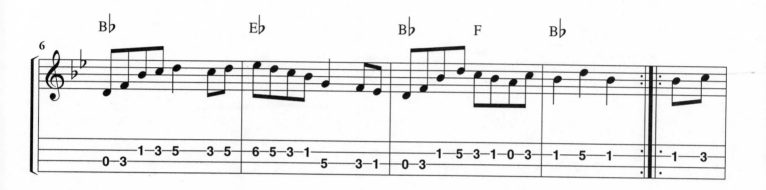

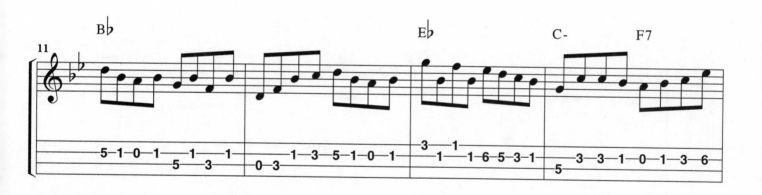

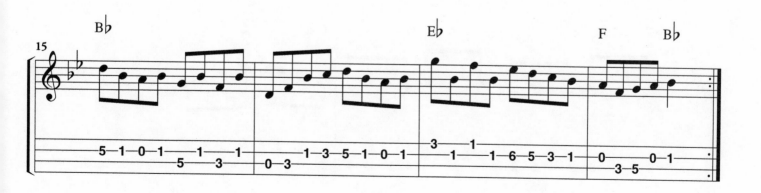

Murphy's Hornpipe

Irish Hornpipe

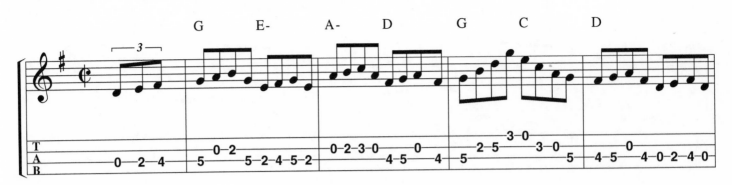

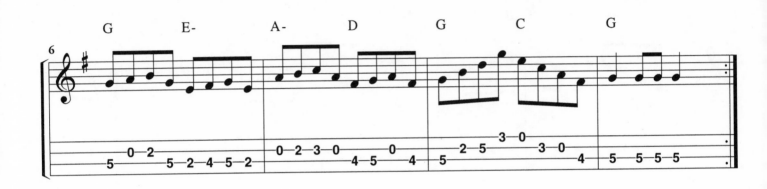

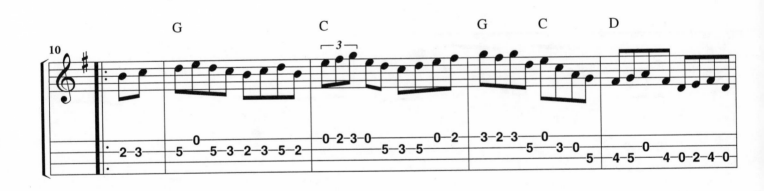

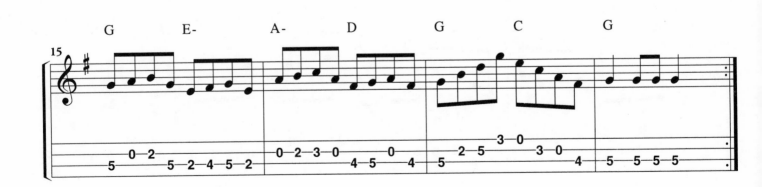

Fisher's Hornpipe

Irish Hornpipe

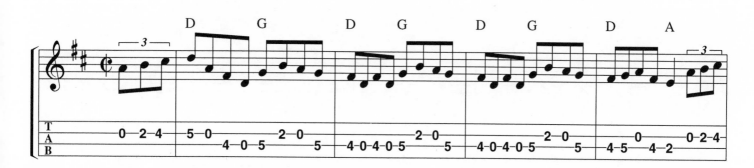

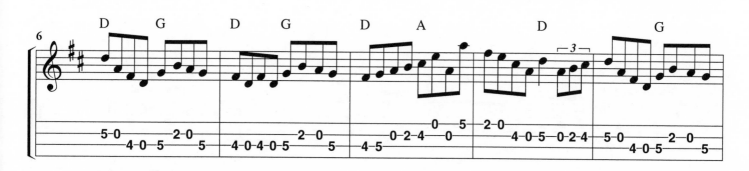

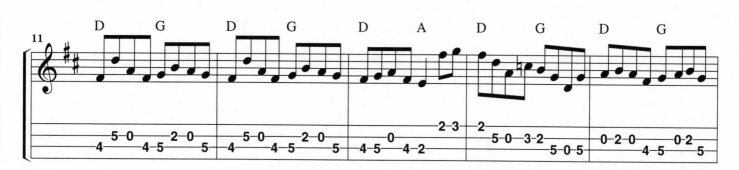

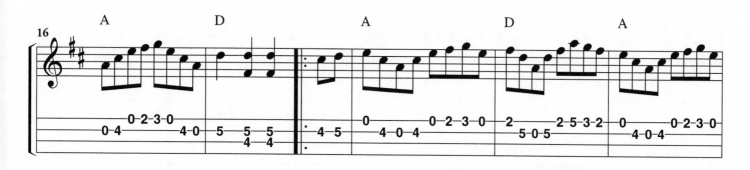

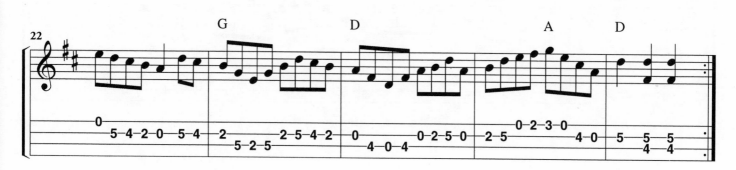

O'Dwyer's Hornpipe

Irish Hornpipe

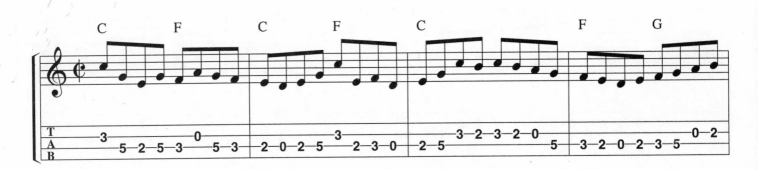

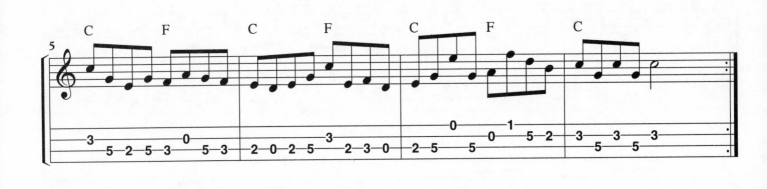

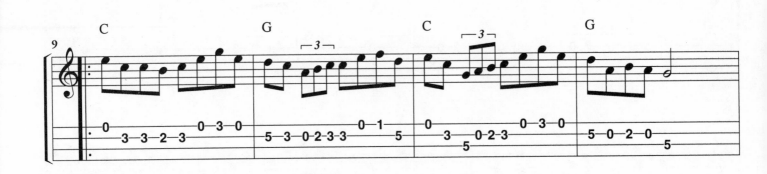

Byrne's Hornpipe

Irish Hornpipe

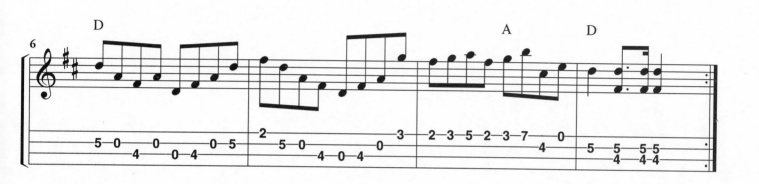

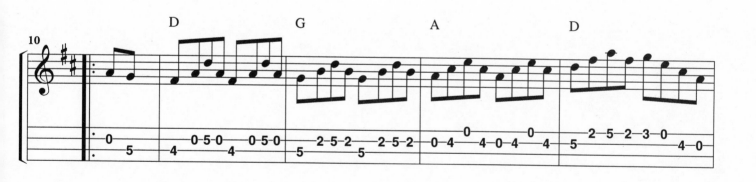

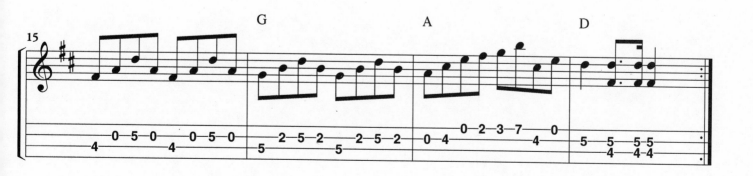

Reels

Sailor on the Rock

Irish Reel

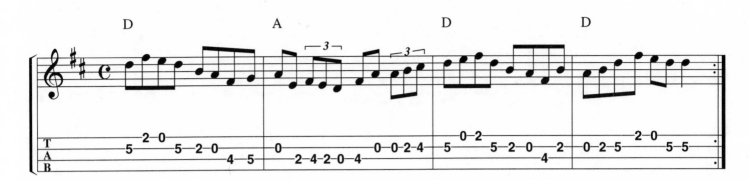

Bare Island

Irish Reel

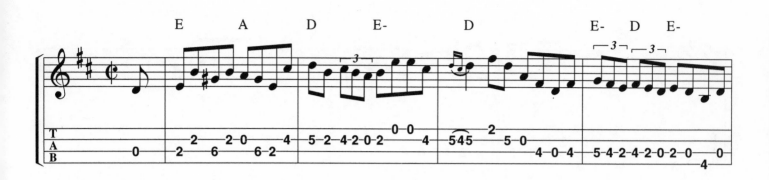

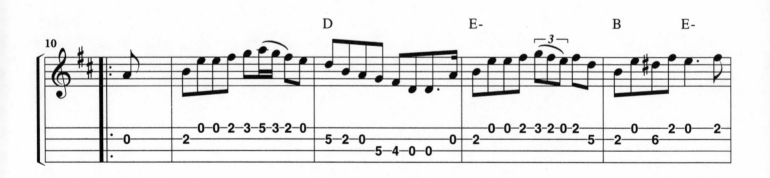

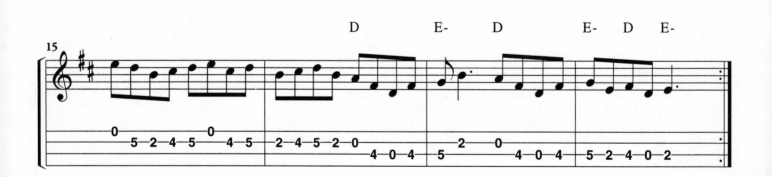

Drowsy Maggie

Irish Reel

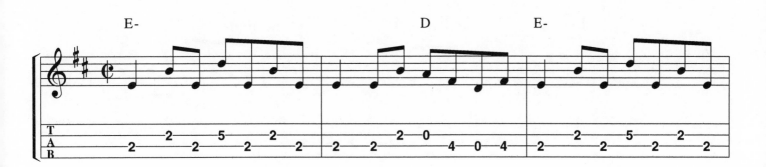

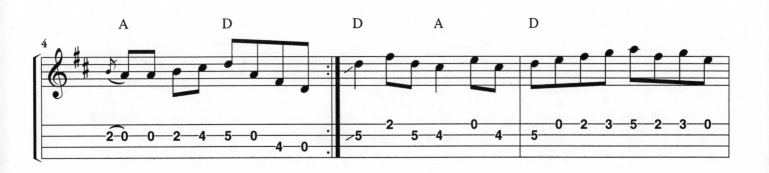

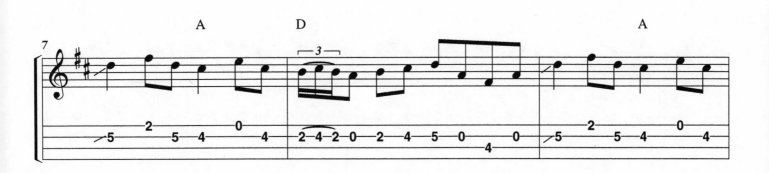

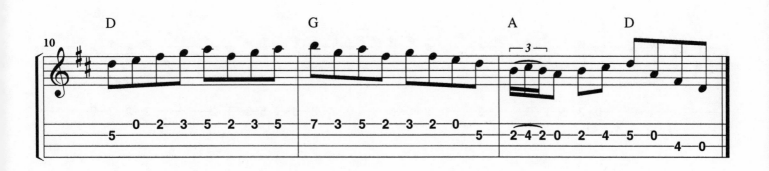

The Reel of Mullinavat

Irish Reel

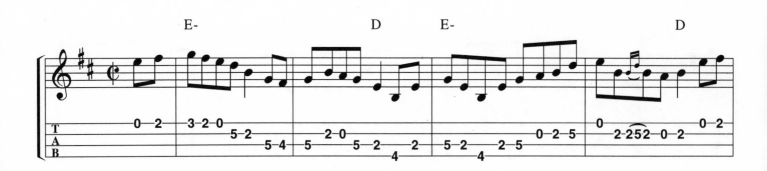

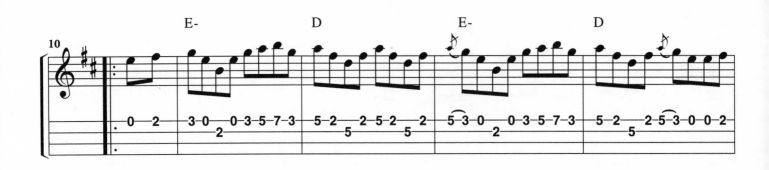

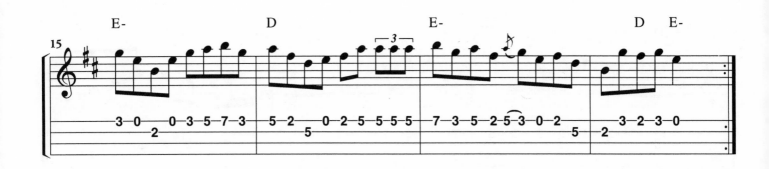

Father Kelly's

Irish Reel

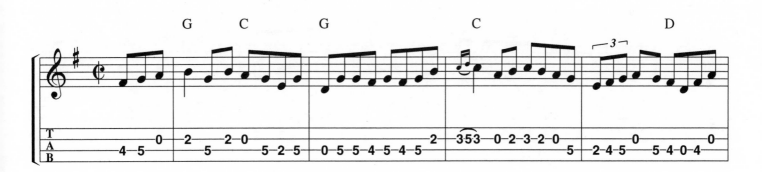

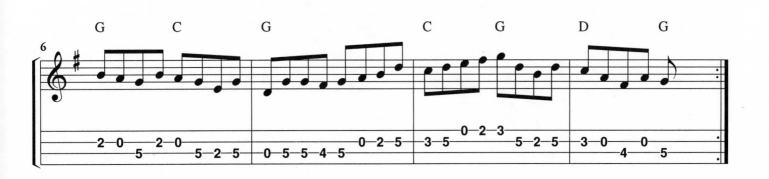

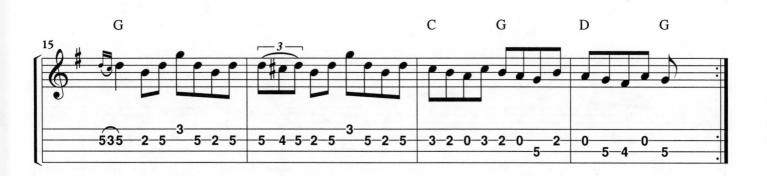

The Irishman's Toast

Irish Reel

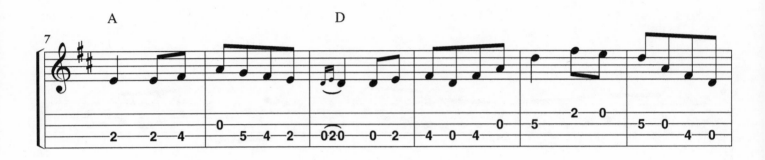

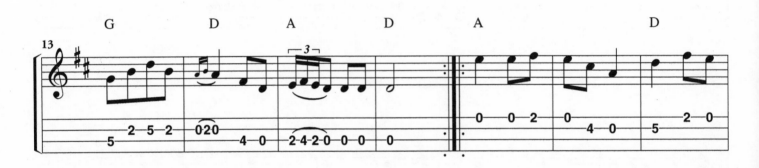

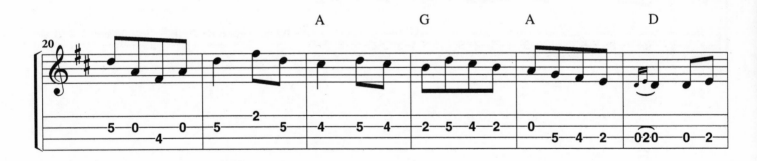

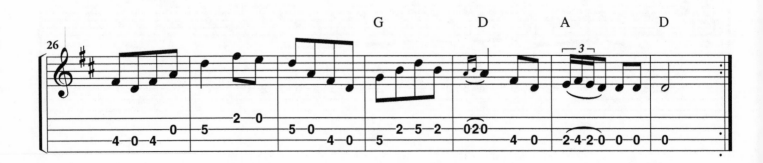

Paddy Ryan's Dream

Irish Reel

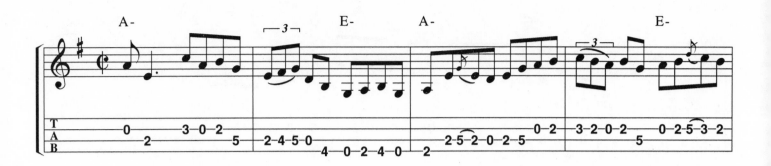

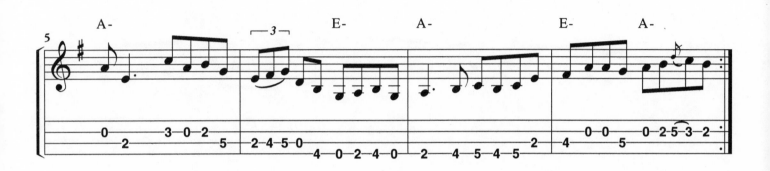

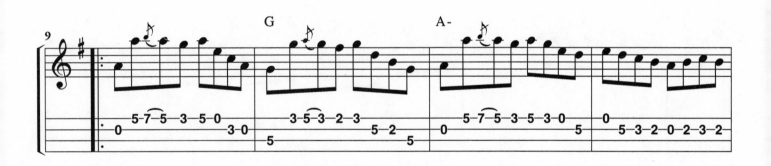

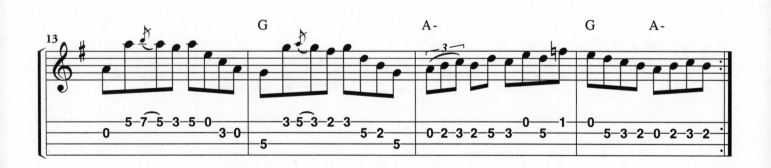

The Green Fields to America

Irish Reel

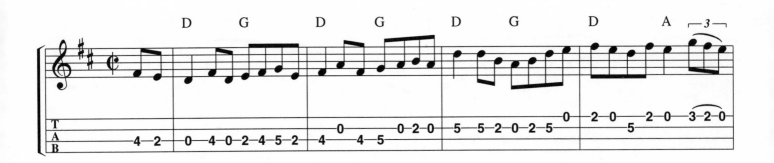

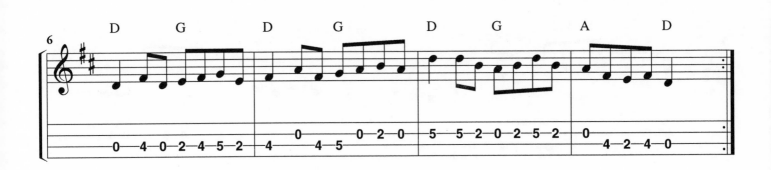

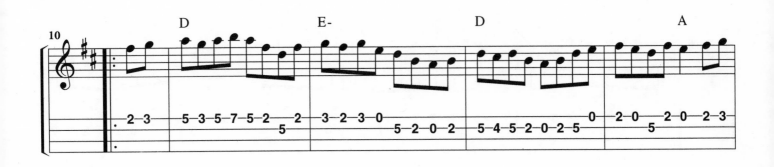

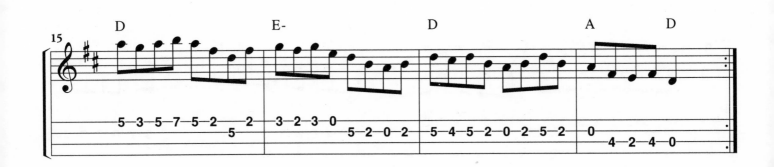

Thompson's Reel

Irish Reel

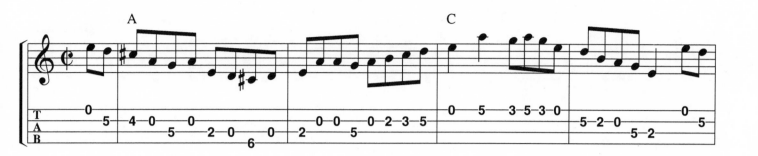

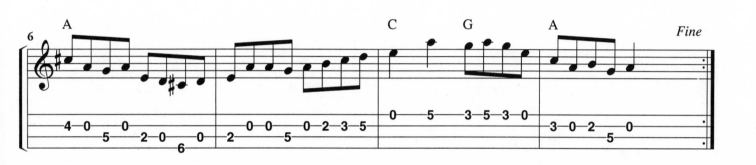

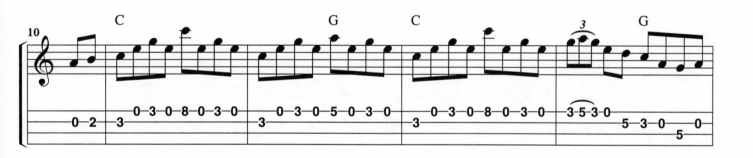

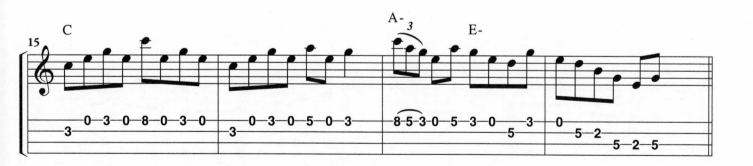

A Galway Reel

Irish Reel

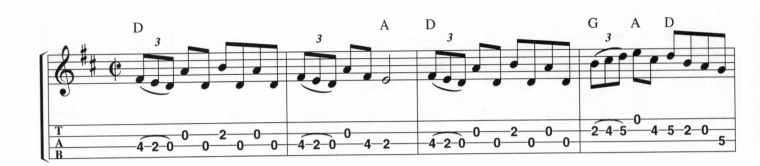

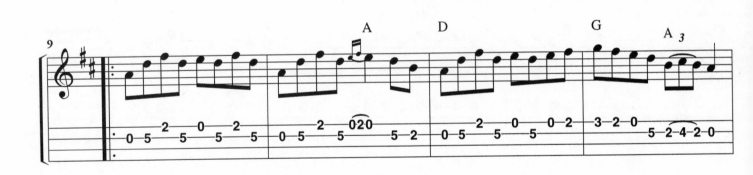

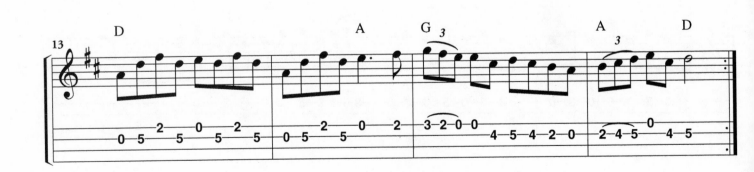

Green Grow the Rushes - O

Irish Reel

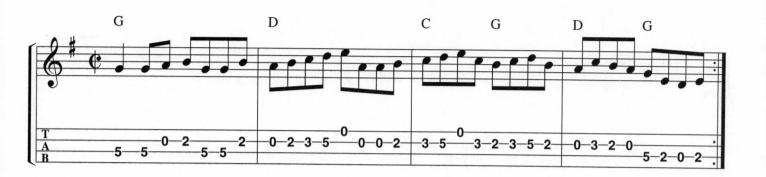

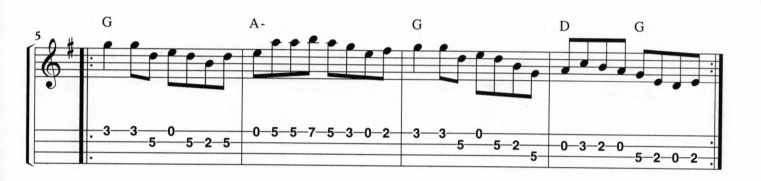

Toss the Feather's

Irish Reel

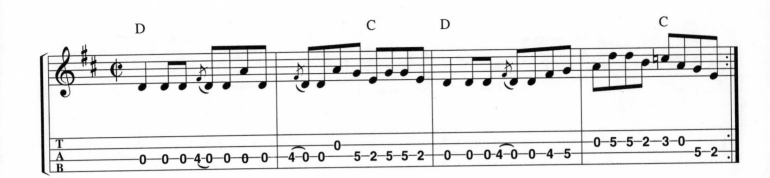

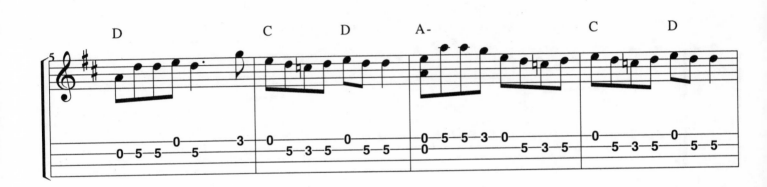

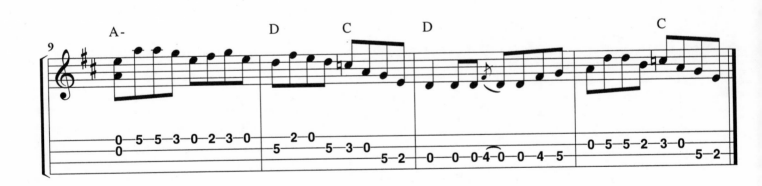

Old Mother Flanagan

Irish Reel

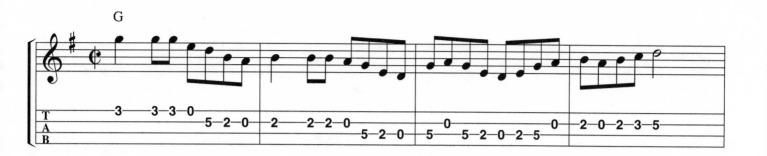

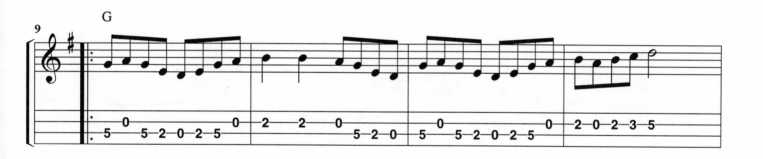

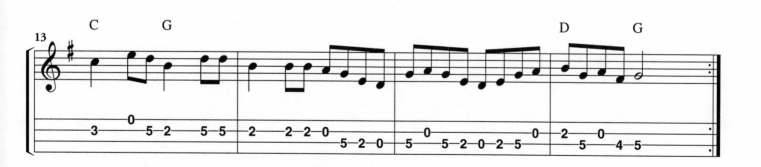

The Blackthorn Stick

Irish Reel

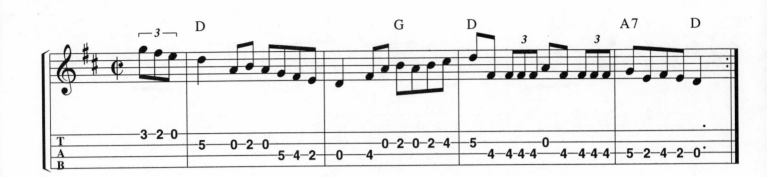

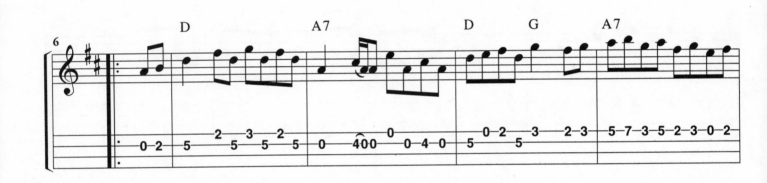

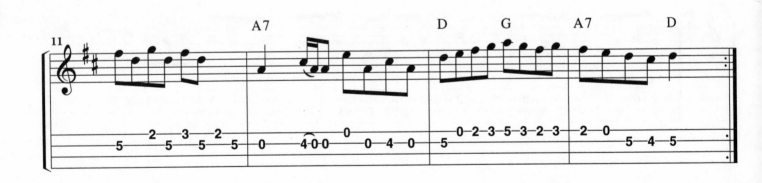

The Eight and Forty Sisters

Irish Reel

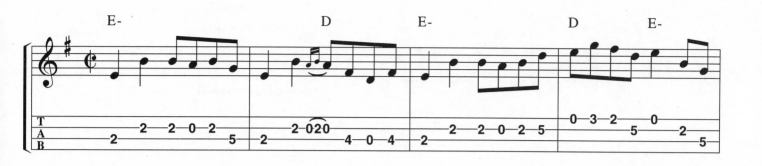

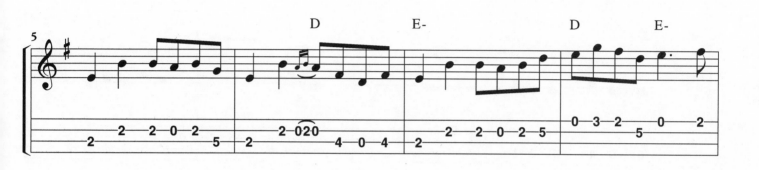

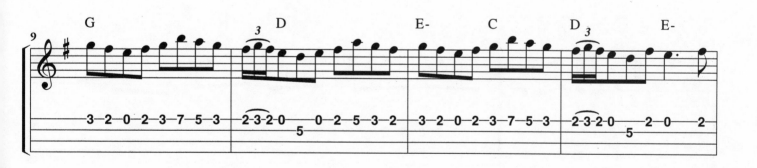

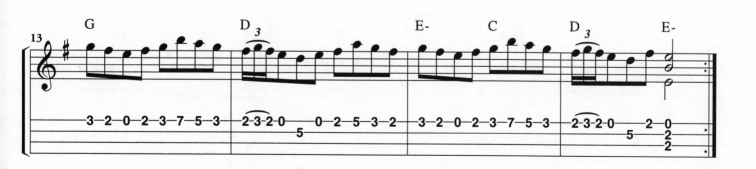

The Trip to Durrow

Irish Reel

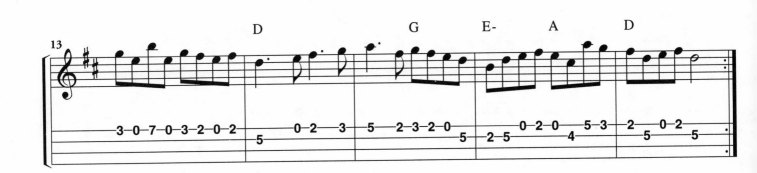

The Tinkers Wife

Irish Reel

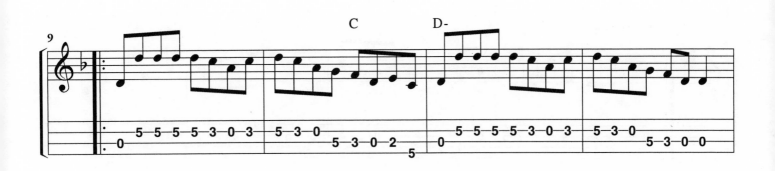

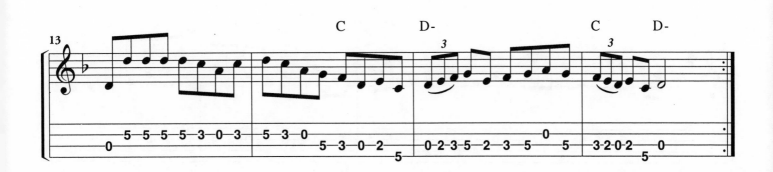

Molony's Reel

Irish Reel

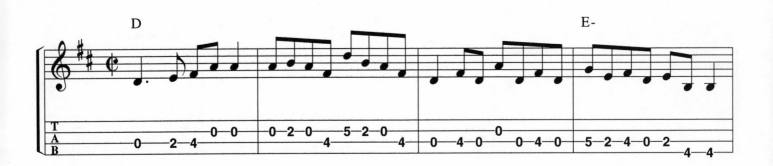

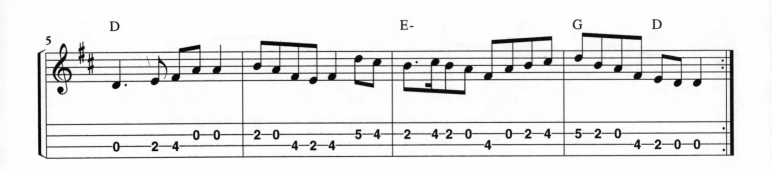

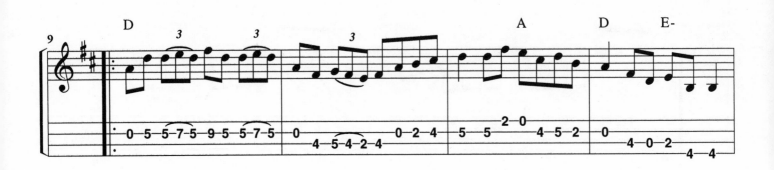

Reel

Irish Reel

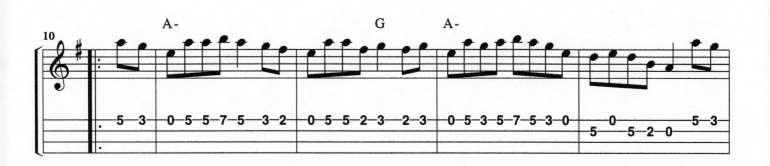

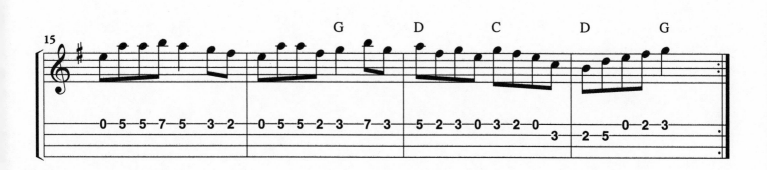

Shannon Breeze

Irish Reel

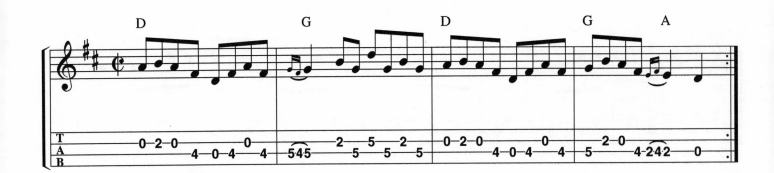

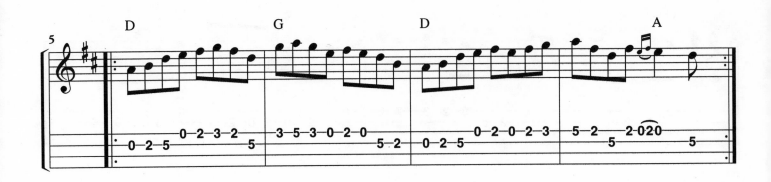

Scottish Music

Airs

Rose Acre

Scottish Air

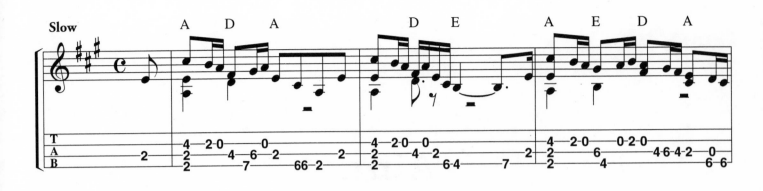

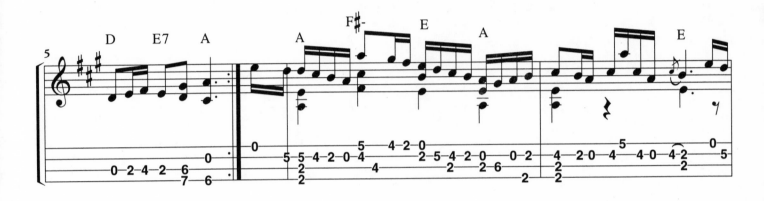

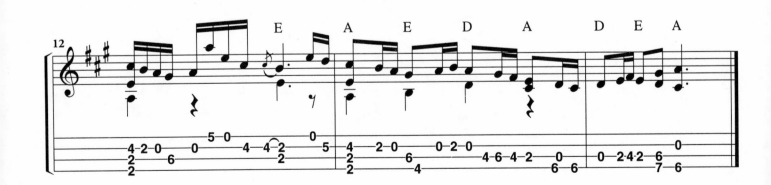

Farewell to Whisky

Scottish Air

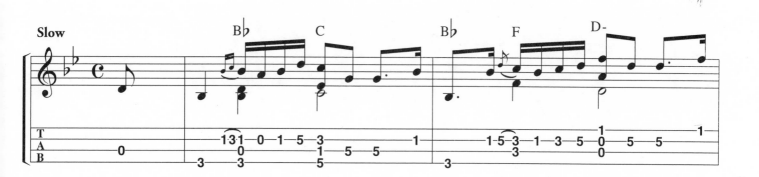

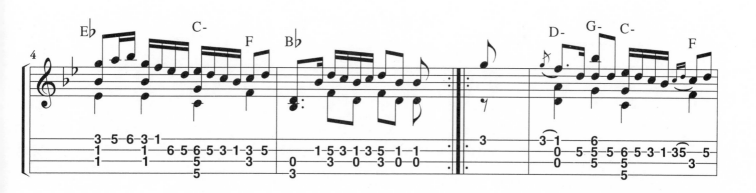

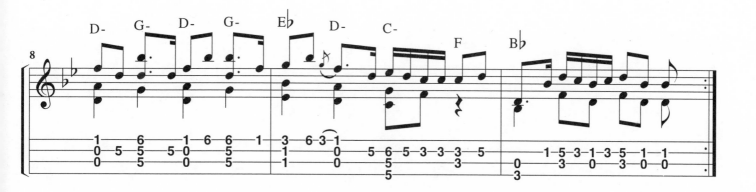

MacGillamun's Oran Mor

Scottish Air

Major Graham of Inchbrakie

Scottish Air

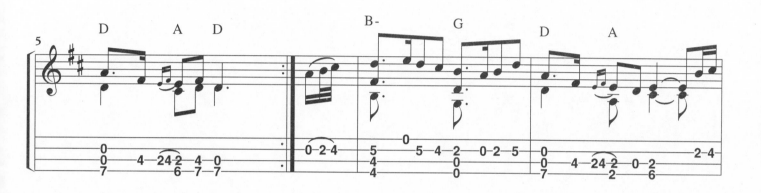

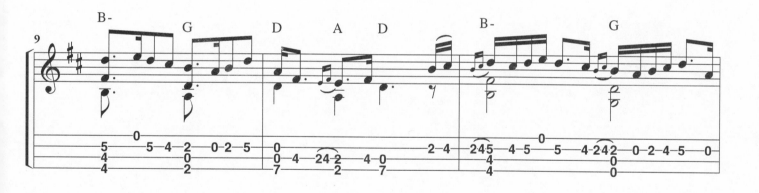

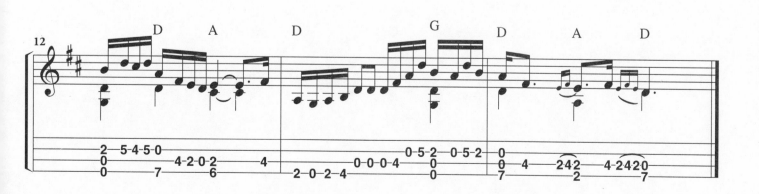

The Nameless Lassie

Scottish Air

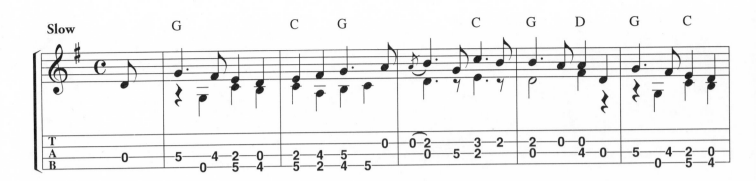

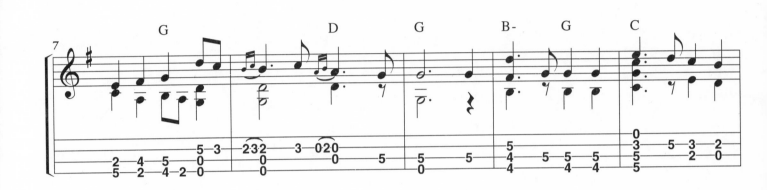

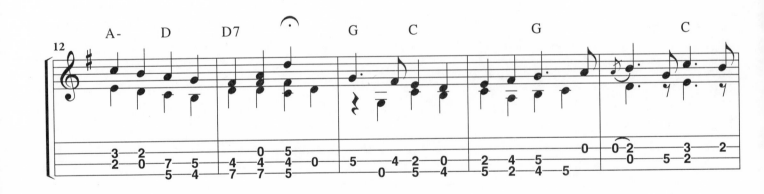

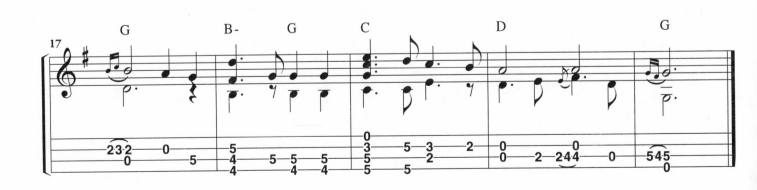

The Rose-Bud of Allenvalle

Scottish Air

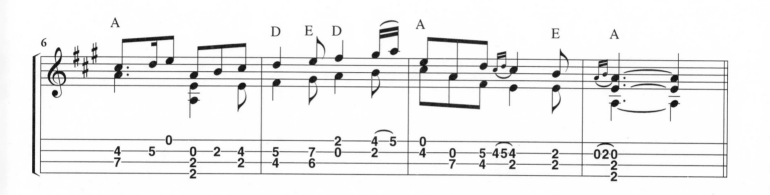

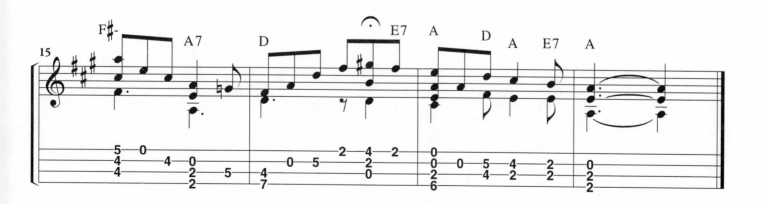

The Hills of Lorne

Scottish Air

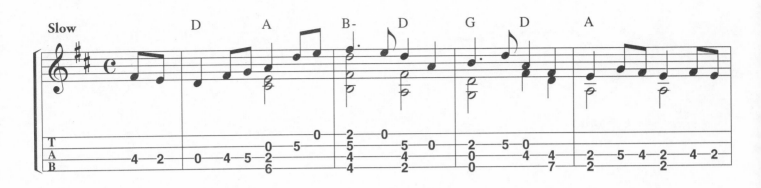

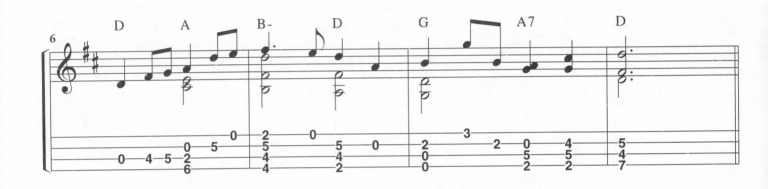

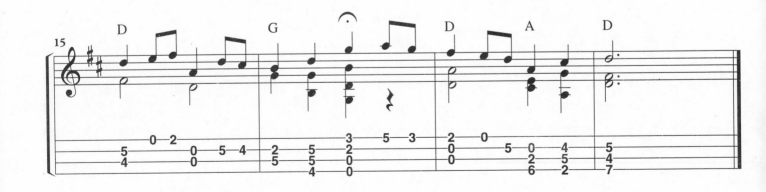

Mary, Young and Fair

Scottish Air

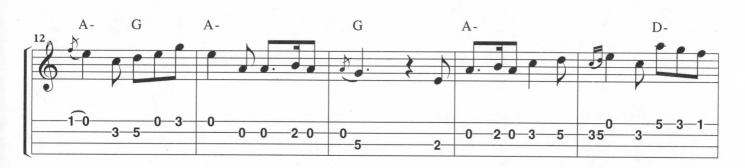

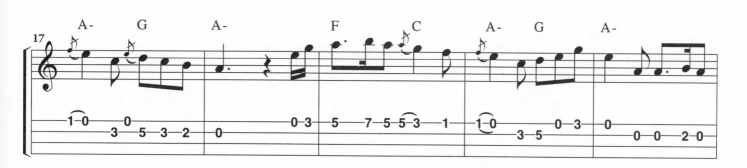

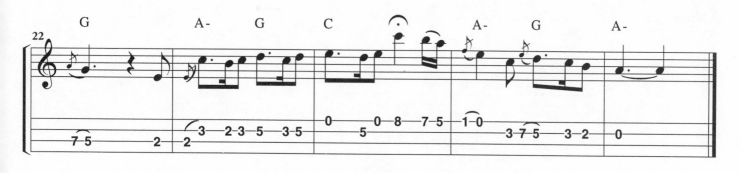

MacPherson's Rant

Scottish Air

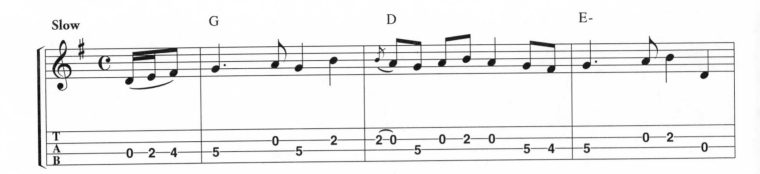

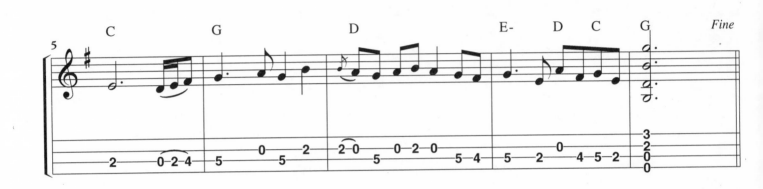

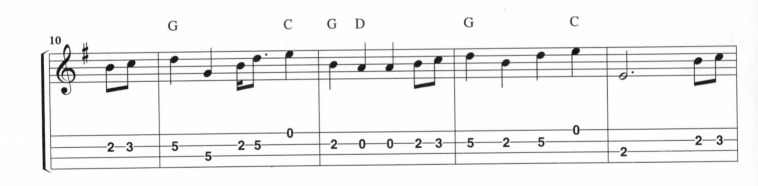

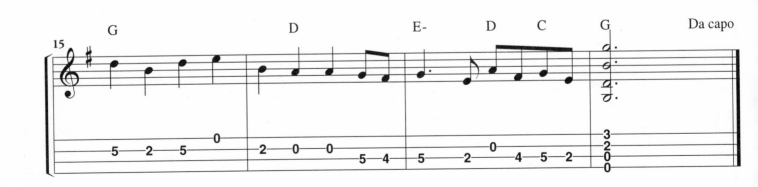

The Cradle Song

Scottish Air

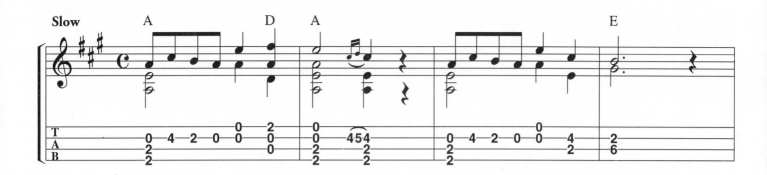

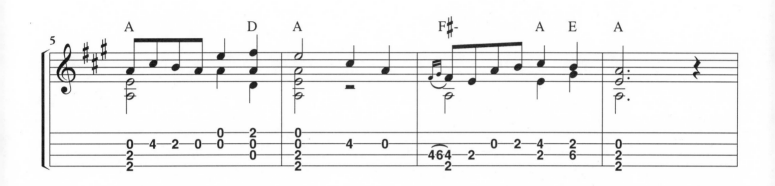

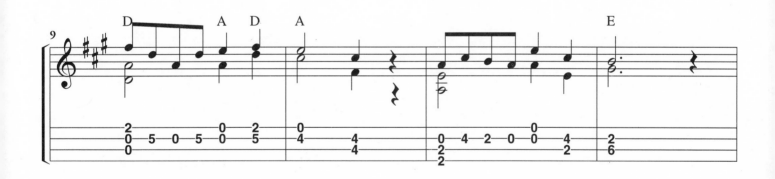

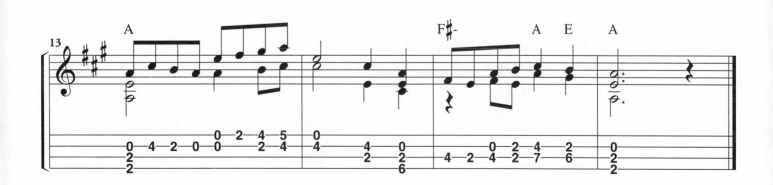

Strathspeys

The Banks of Loch Ness

Strathspey

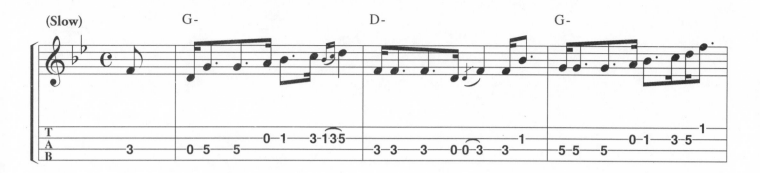

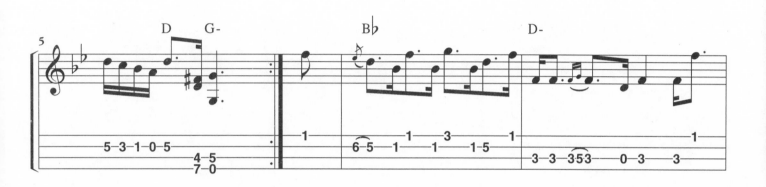

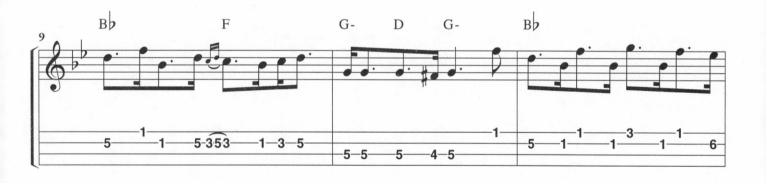

Hon. Miss Elliot

Strathspey

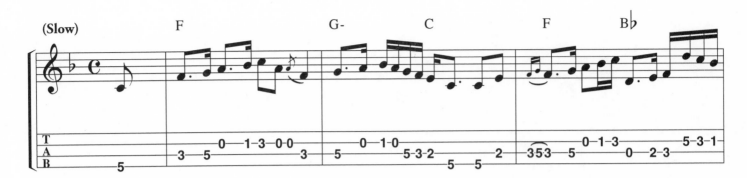

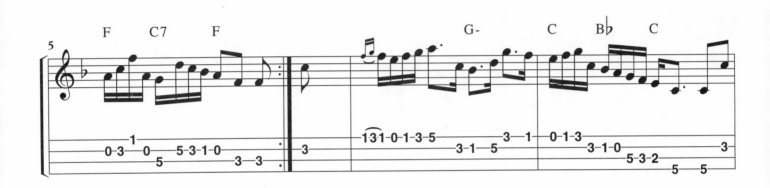

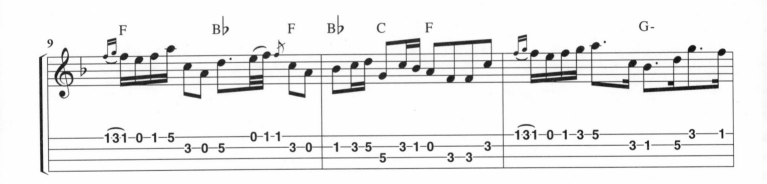

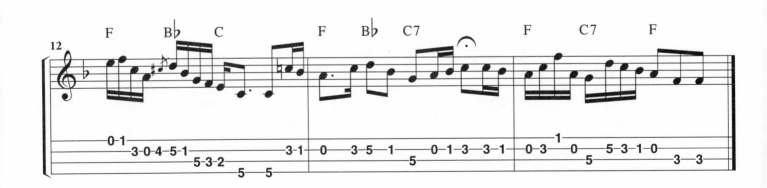

Miss Sarah Drummond of Perth

Scottish Strathspey

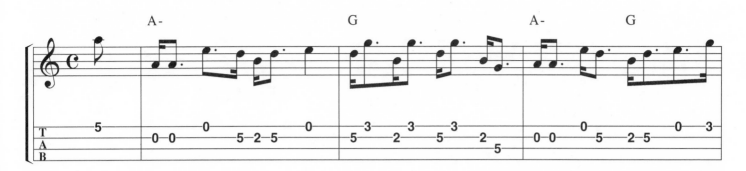

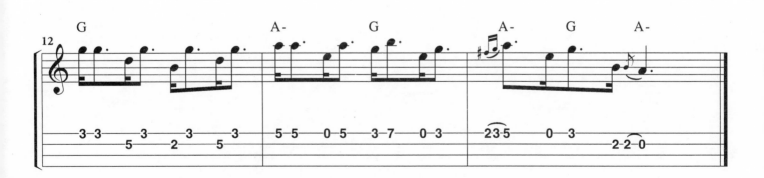

The Ewie with the Crooked Horn

Scottish Strathspey

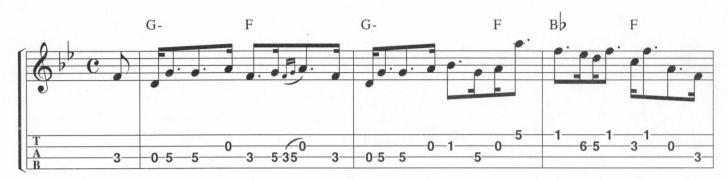

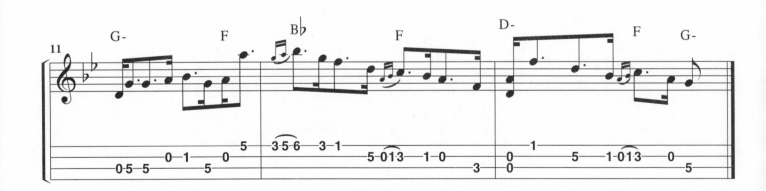

Glenlivet Whisky

Scottish Strathspey

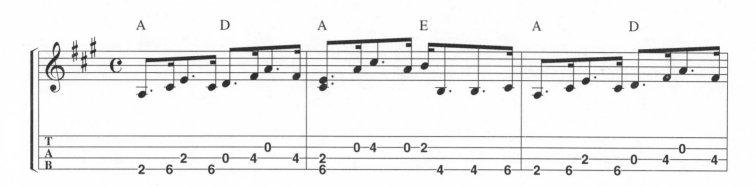

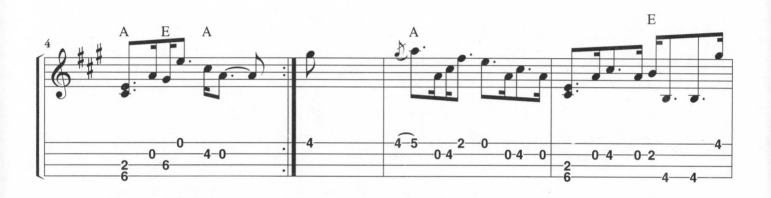

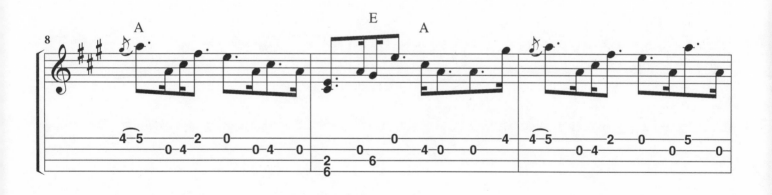

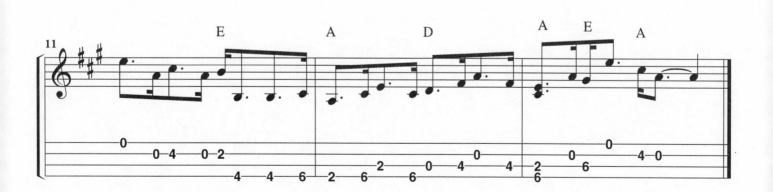

The Brig O'Potarch

Scottish Strathspey

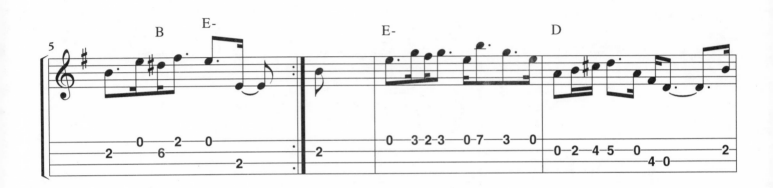

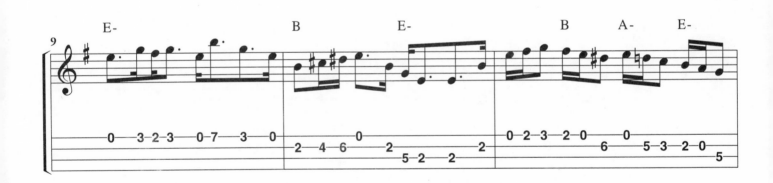

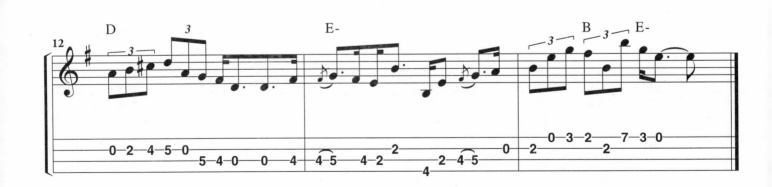

The Devil's in the Kitchen

Scottish Strathspey

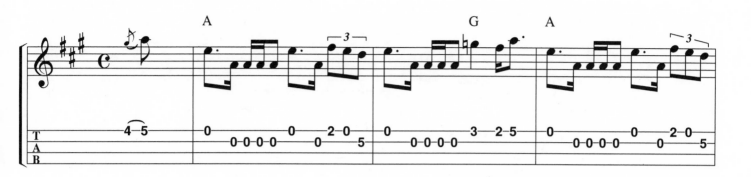

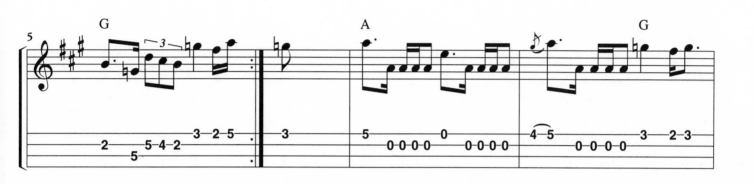

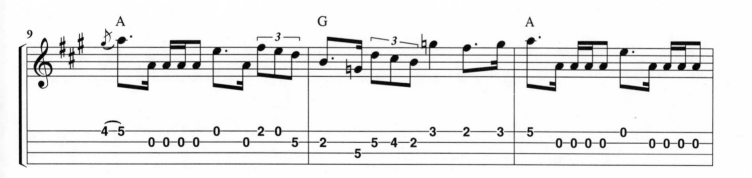

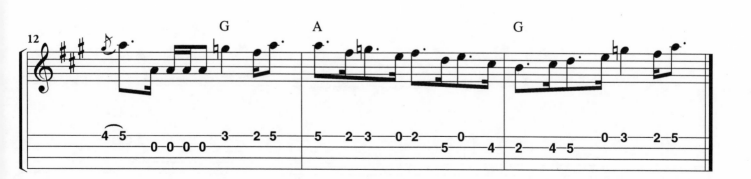

The Braes O'Mar

Scottish Strathspey

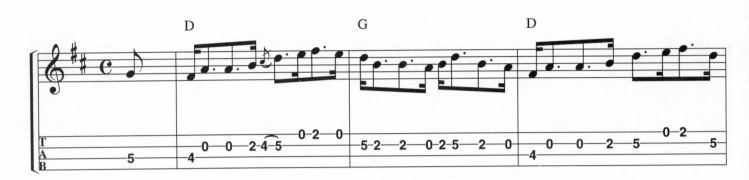

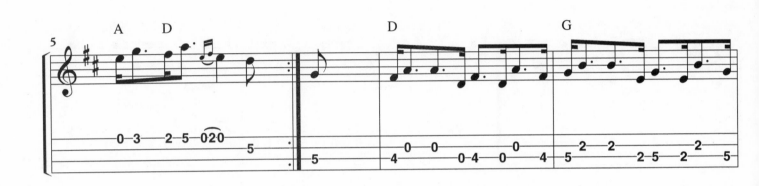

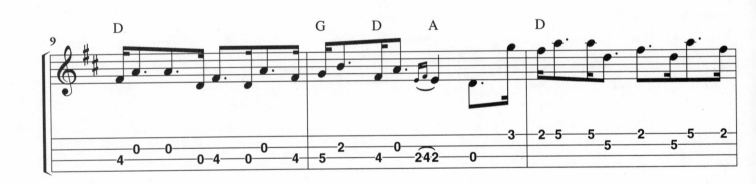

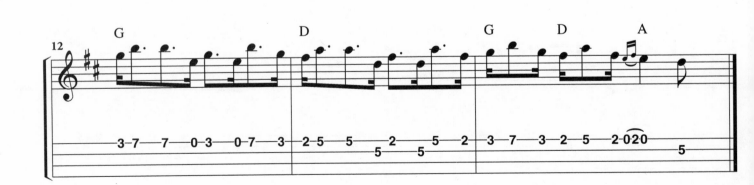

Carron Water

Scottish Strathspey

Heilan Donald Kissed Kitty

Scottish Strathspey

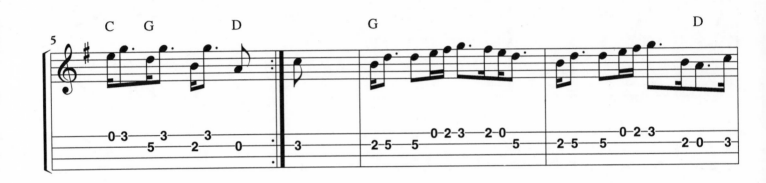

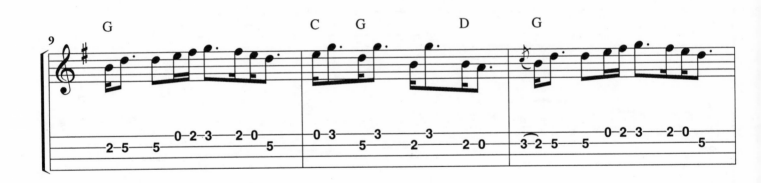

Jígs

The Haymakers

Scottish Jig

Newcastle Bridge

Scottish Jig

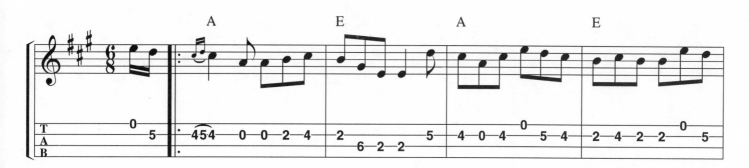

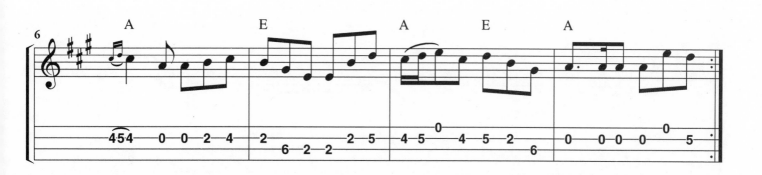

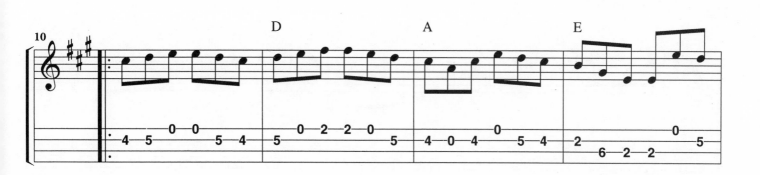

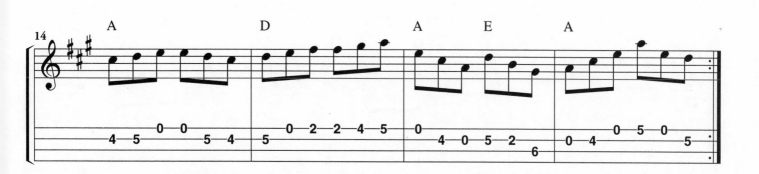

Middling, Thank You

Scottish Jig

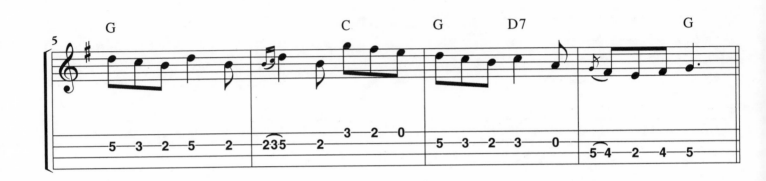

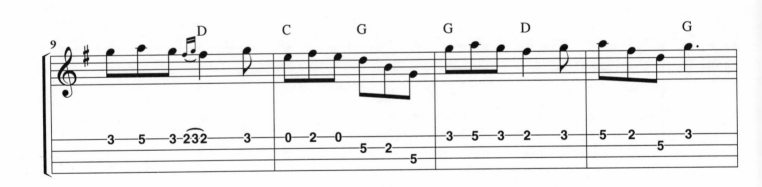

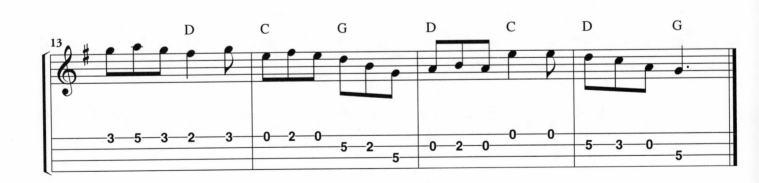

Miss Sally Hunter of Thurston

Scottish Jig

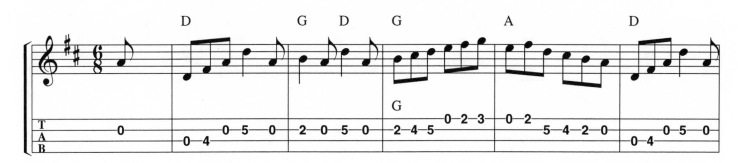

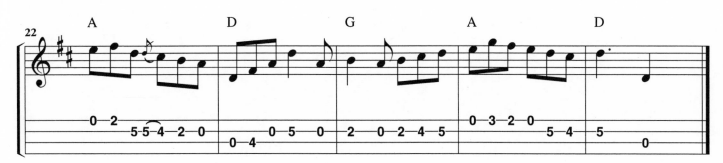

Miss Ann Cameron of Balvenie

Scottish Jig
Slip Jig

Drops of Brandy

Scottish Jig
Slip Jig

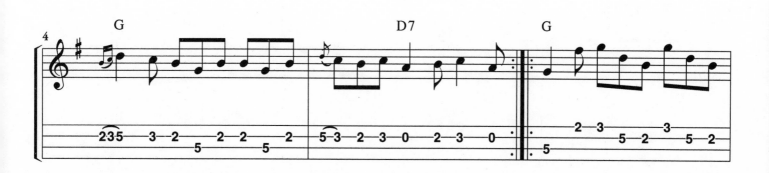

Drummond Castle

Scottish Jig

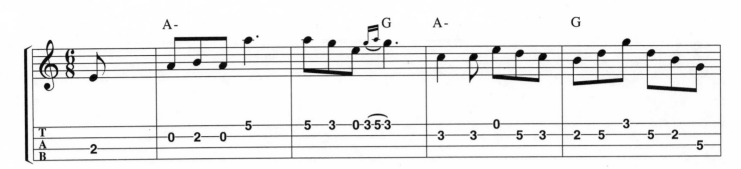

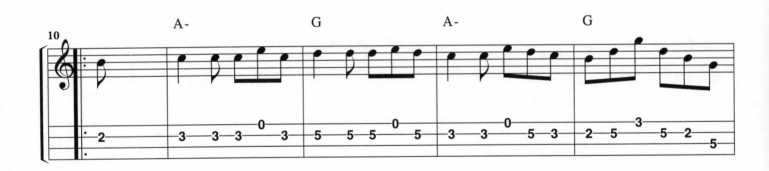

Hamilton House

Scottish Jig

Lamb Skinnet

Scottish Jig

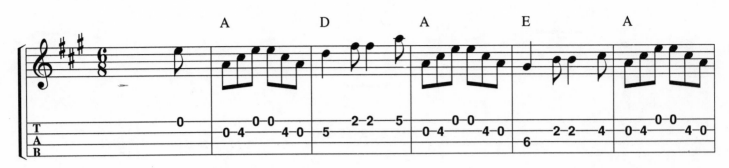

The Deuks Dang O'er My Daddie

Scottish Jig

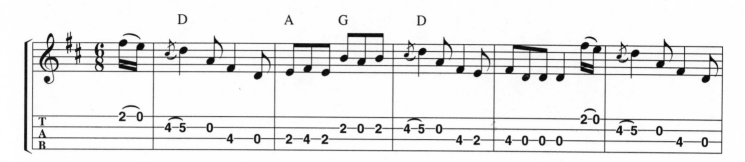

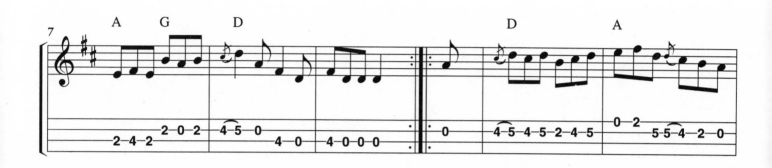

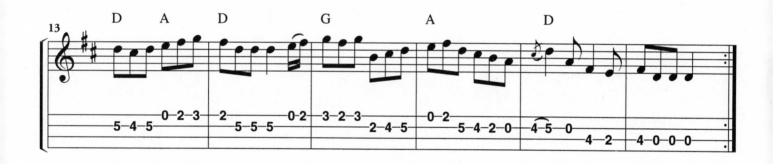

Country Dances

The Flowers of Edinburgh

Scottish Country Dance

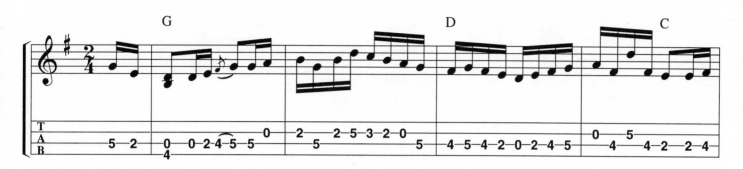

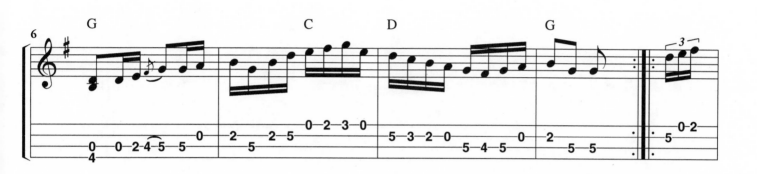

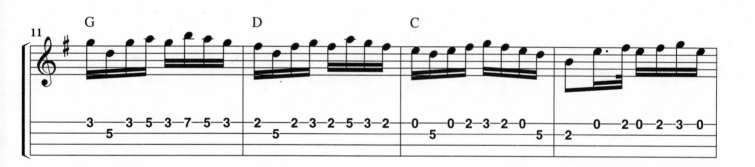

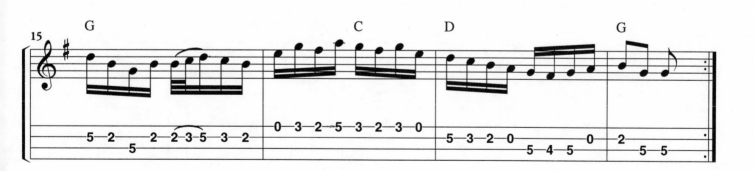

Staten Island

Scottish Country Dance

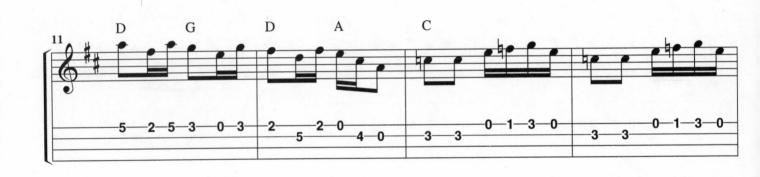

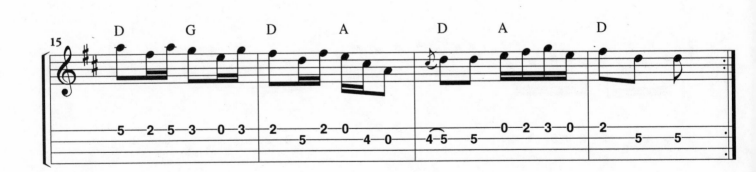

The Marchfield Brae Scots Measure

Scottish Country Dance

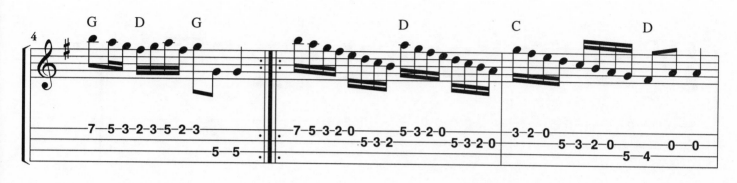

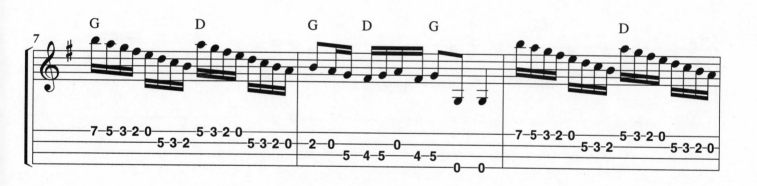

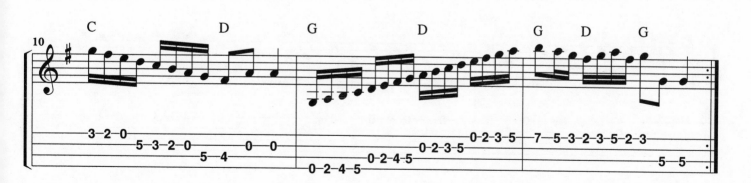

Meg Merrilees

Scottish Country Dance

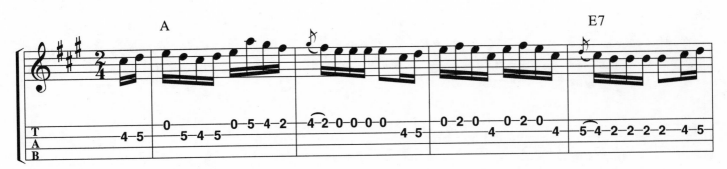

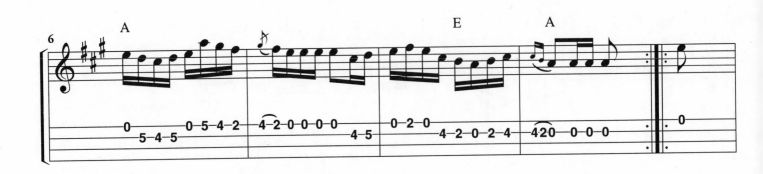

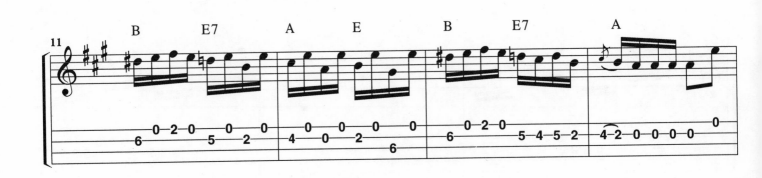

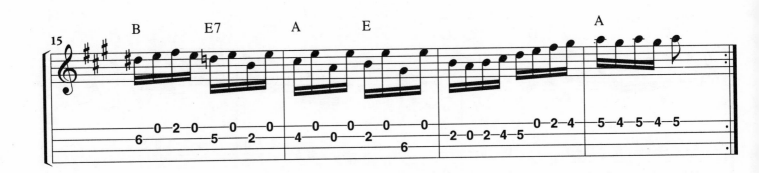

Petronella

Scottish Country Dance

The Soldiers Joy

Scottish Country Dance

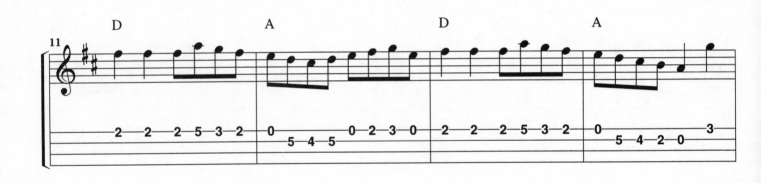

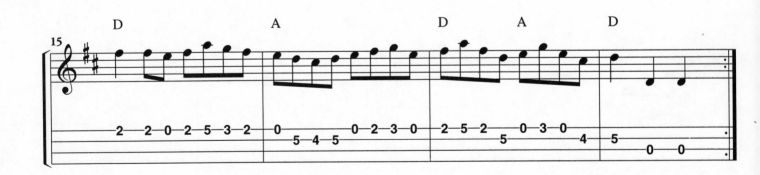

Speed the Plough

Scottish Country Dance

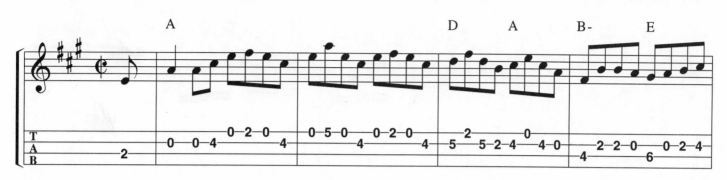

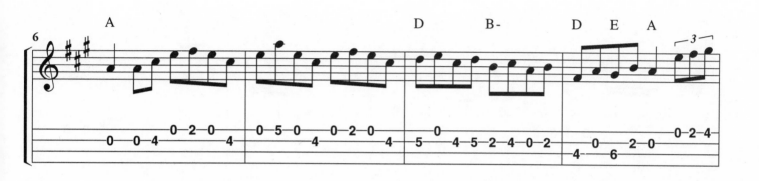

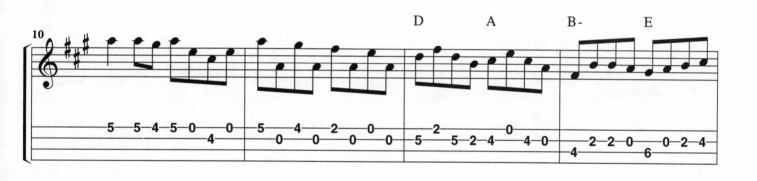

The Cairdin' O'T

Scottish Country Dance

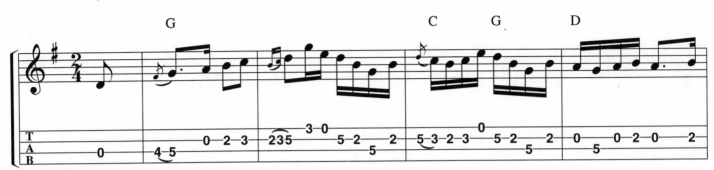

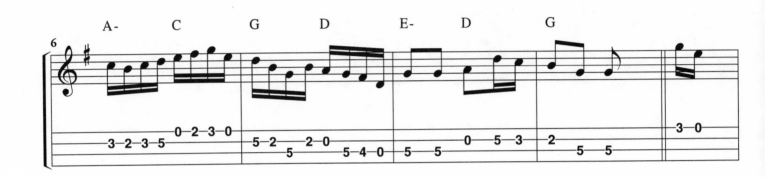

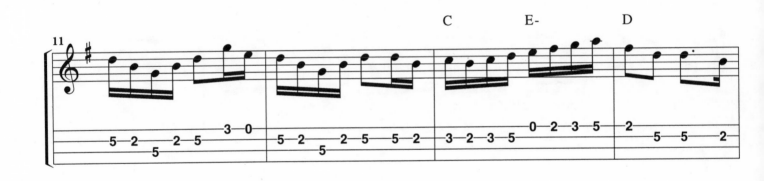

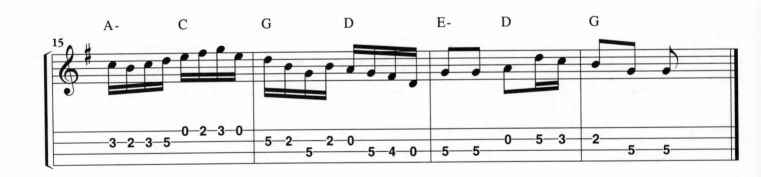

Johnnie in Nether Mains

Scottish Country Dance

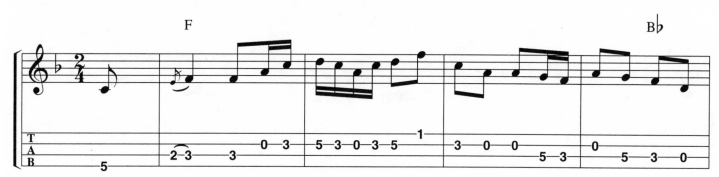

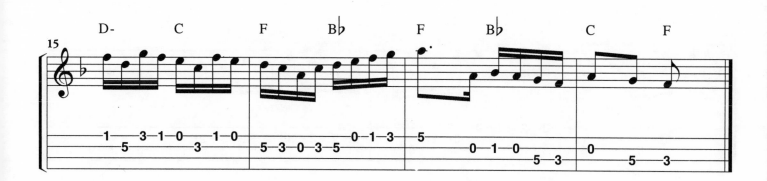

The East Neuk O'Fife

Scottish Country Dance

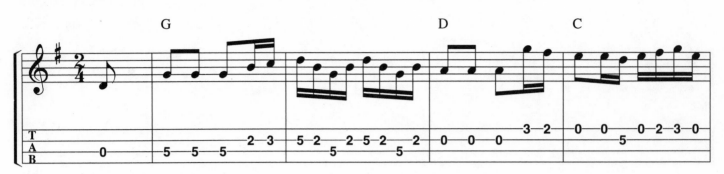

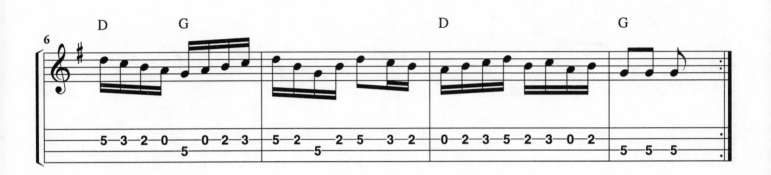

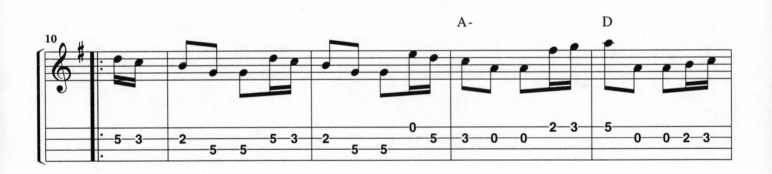

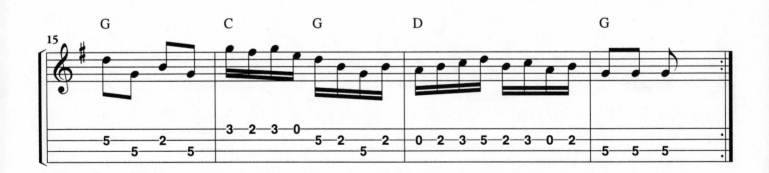

Hornpipes

The High Level Hornpipe

Scottish Hornpipe

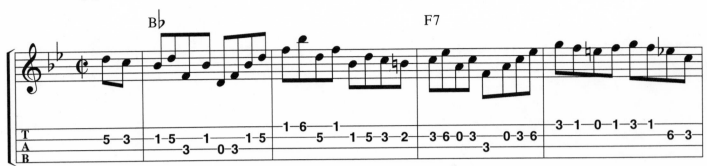

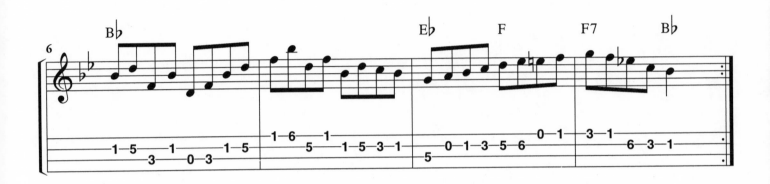

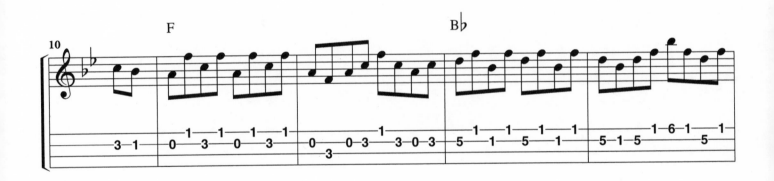

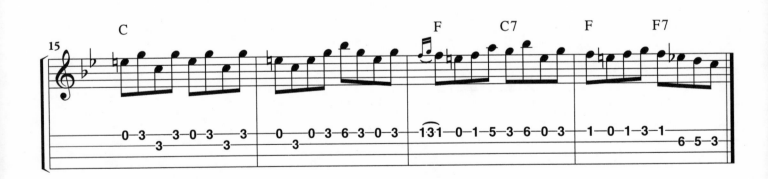

The Newcastle Hornpipe

Scottish Hornpipe

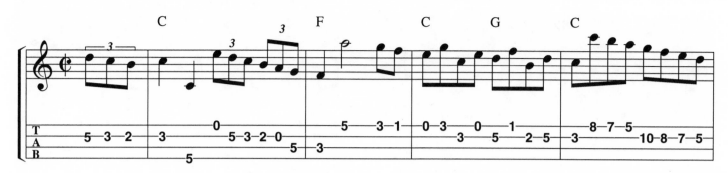

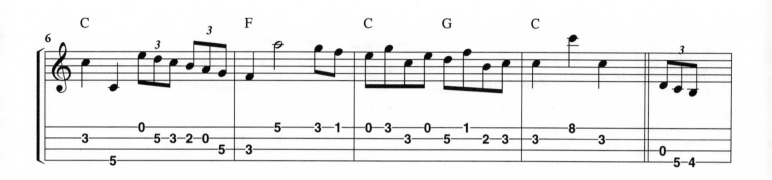

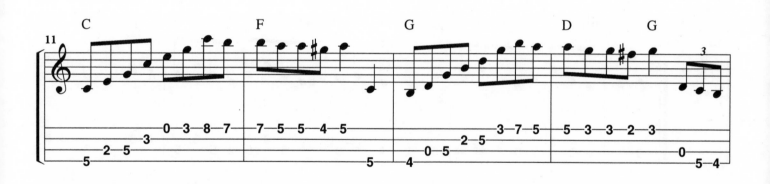

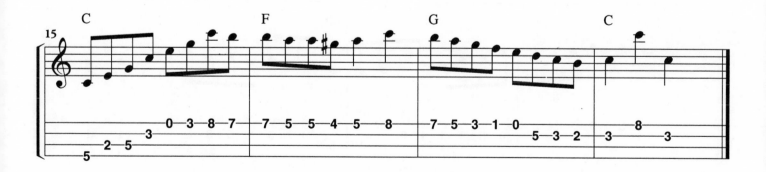

The College Hornpipe

Scottish Hornpipe

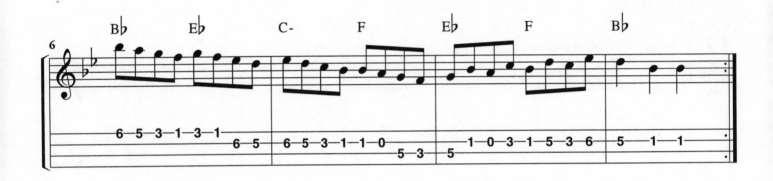

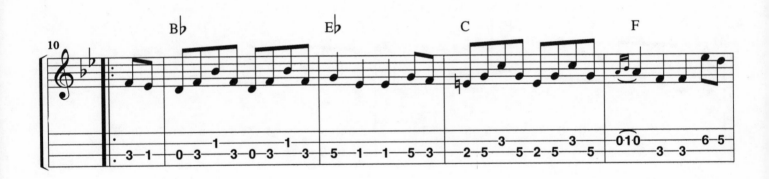

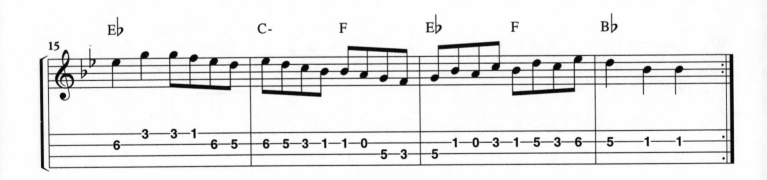

Admiral Nelson

Scottish Hornpipe

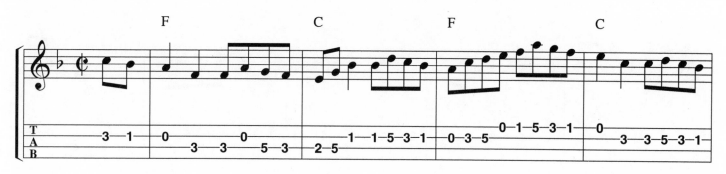

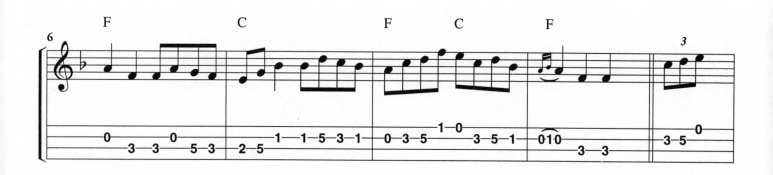

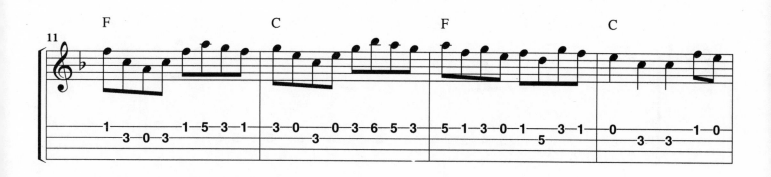

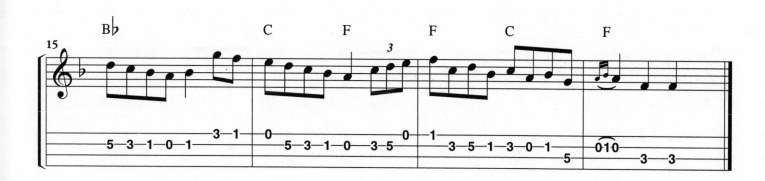

The Bow-Legged Bosun

Scottish Hornpipe

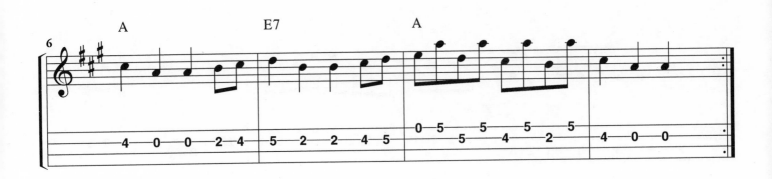

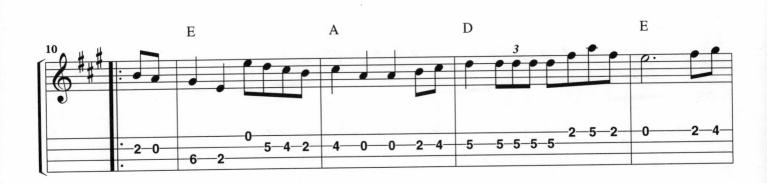

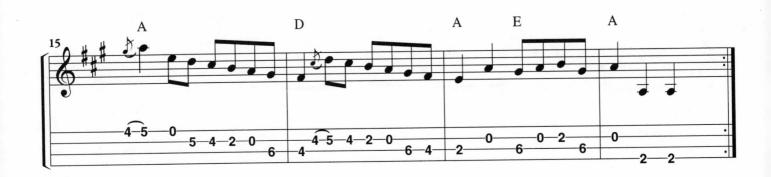

Miss Gayton

Scottish Hornpipe

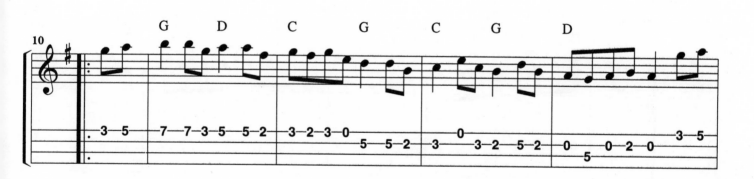

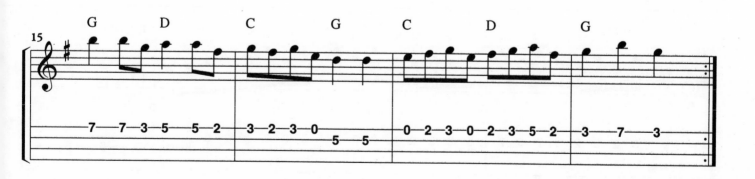

The Lochmaben Hornpipe

Scottish Hornpipe

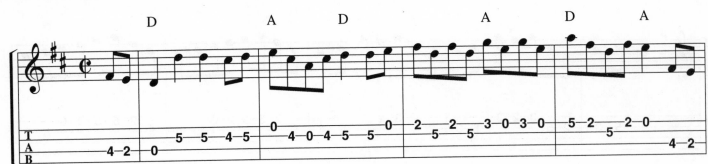

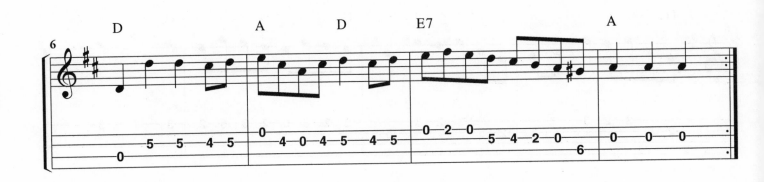

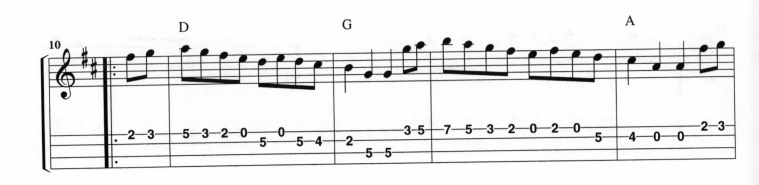

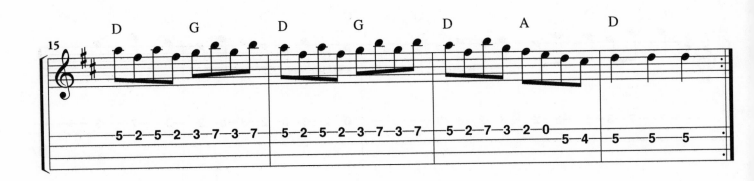

The Rights of Man

Scottish Hornpipe

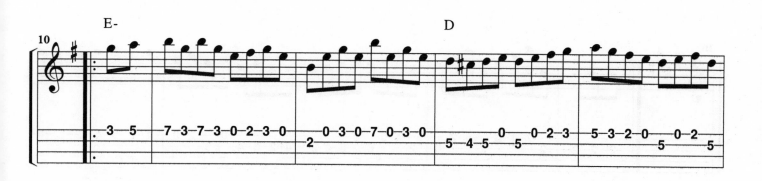

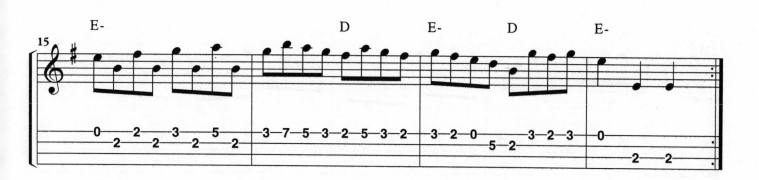

The Hawk Hornpipe

Scottish Hornpipe

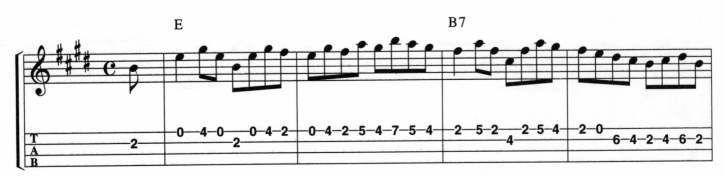

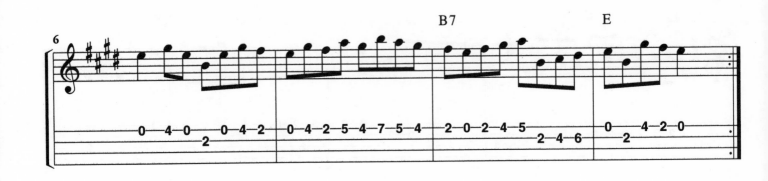

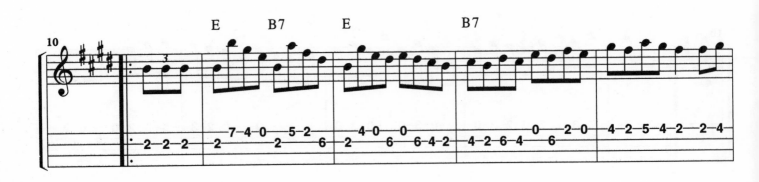

The Trumpet Hornpipe

Scottish Hornpipe

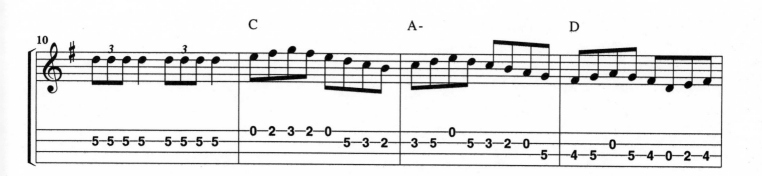

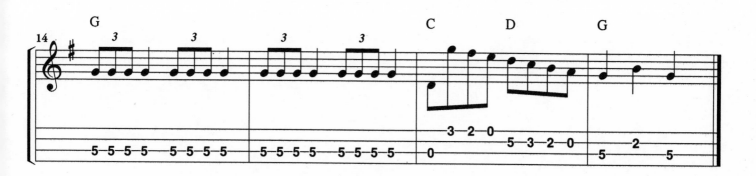

Reels

Colonel McBain

Scottish Reel

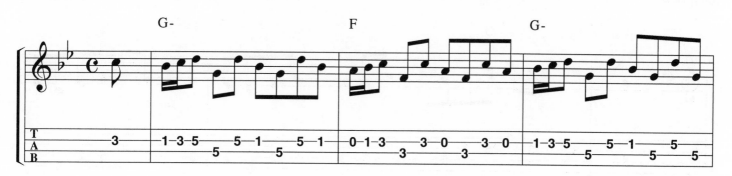

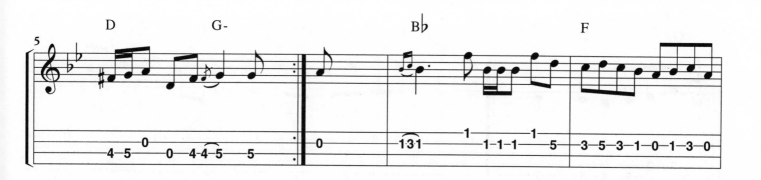

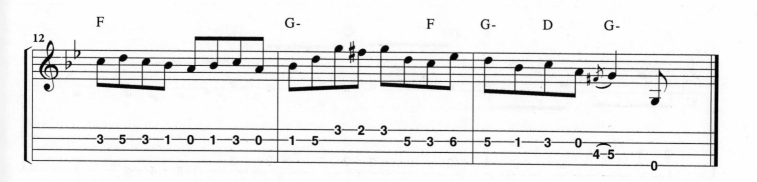

Mrs. Dundas of Arniston

Scottish Reel

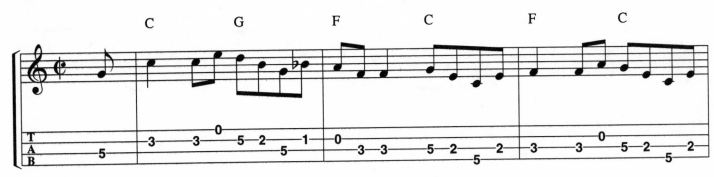

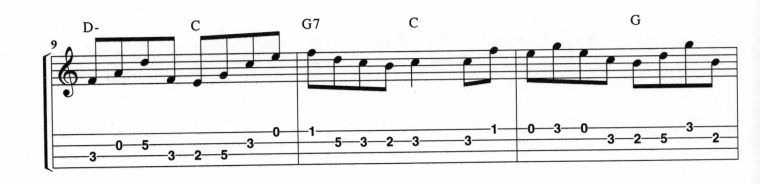

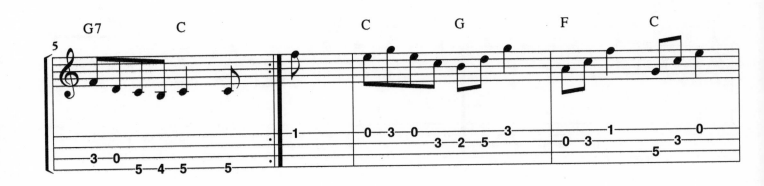

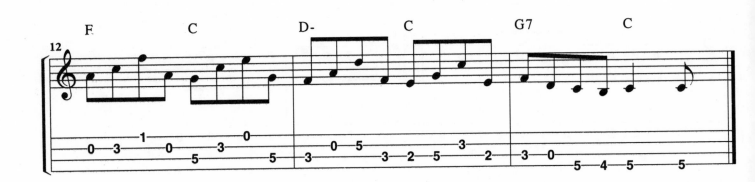

Miss Loudon

Scottish Reel

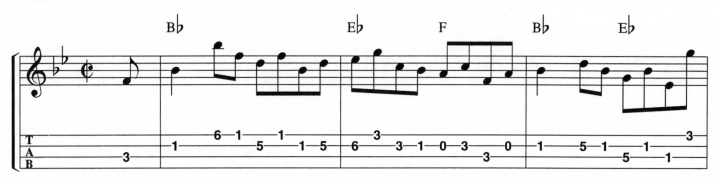

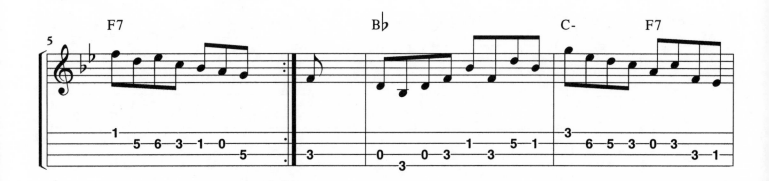

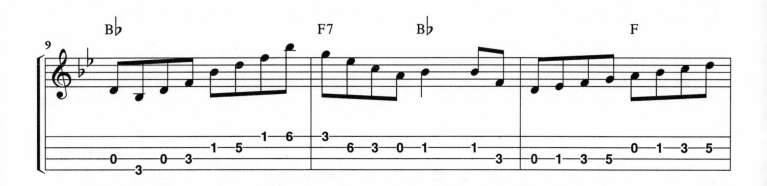

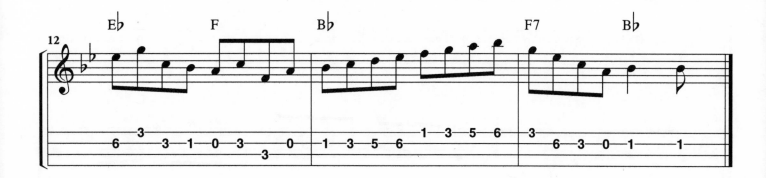

Hon. Mrs. Campbell of Lochnell

Scottish Reel

The Perth Assembly

Scottish Reel

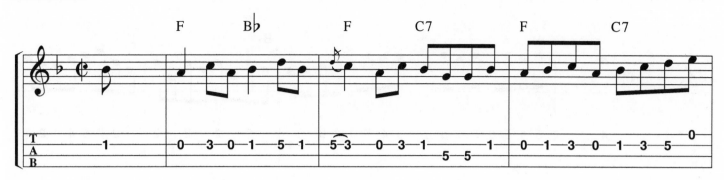

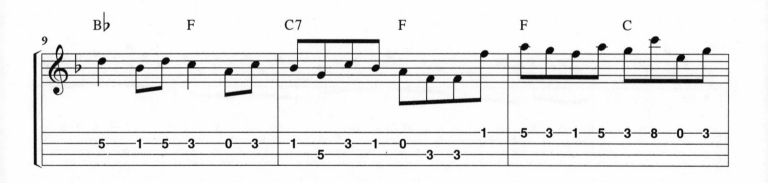

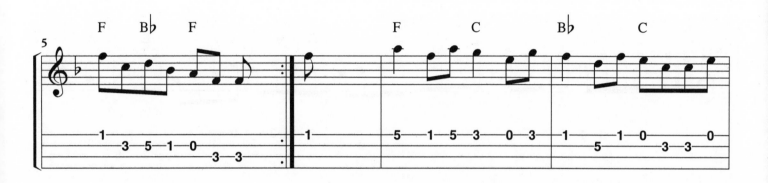

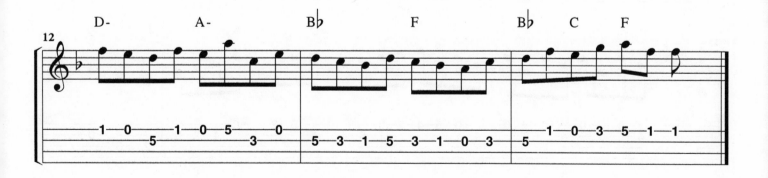

The Deil Amang the Tailors

Scottish Reel

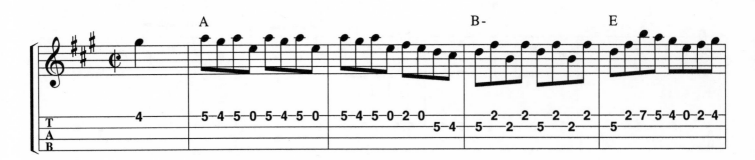

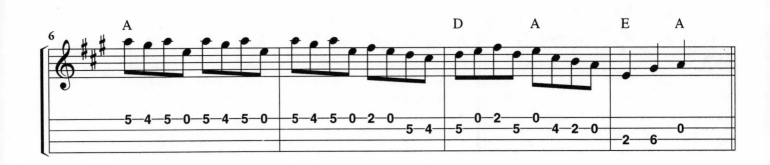

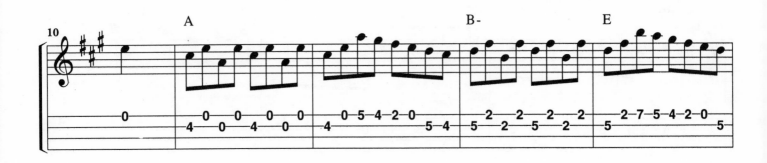

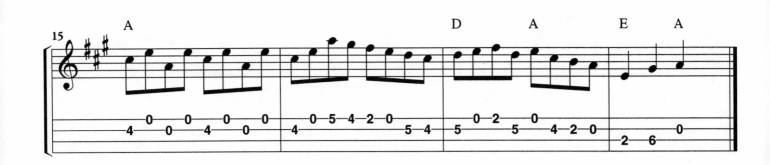

The Black Mill

Scottish Reel

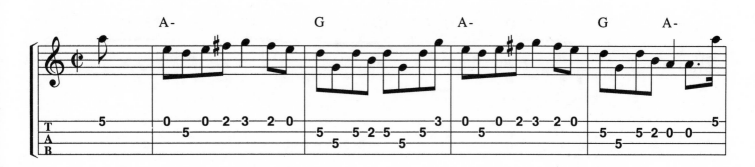

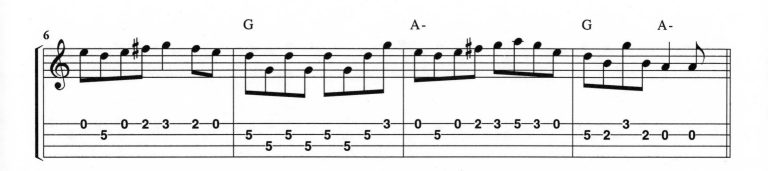

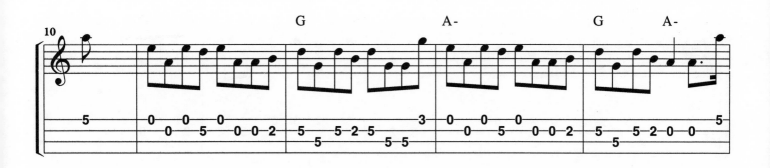

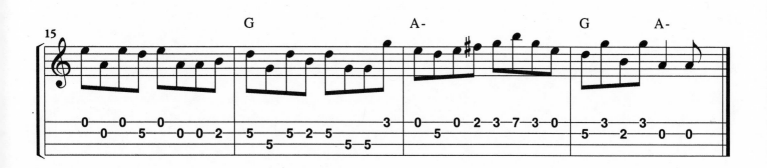

Jack Is Yet Alive

Scottish Reel

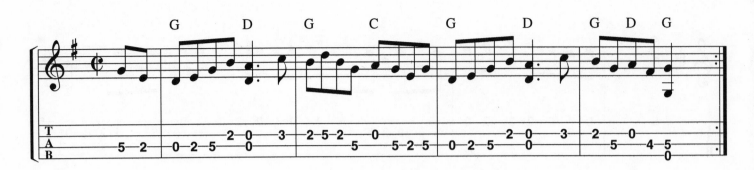

Deil Stick Da Minister

Scottish Reel

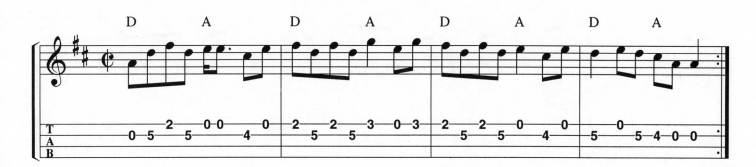

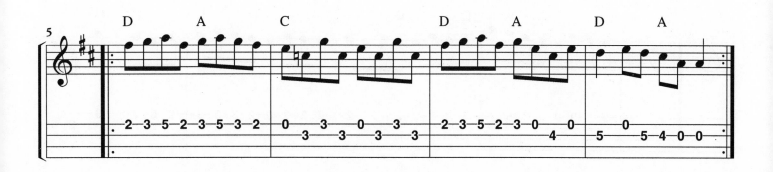

Loch Earn

Scottish Reel

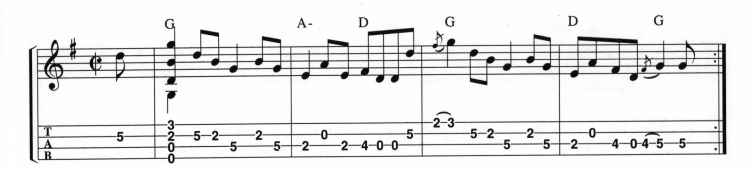

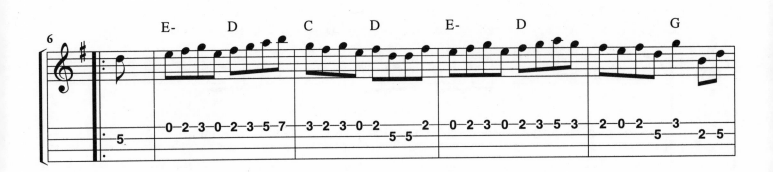

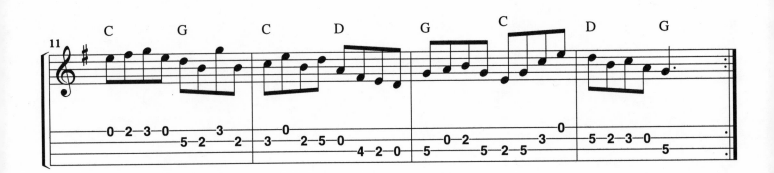